J 921 Henson
Parish, James Robert.
Jim Henson

JIM
HENSON

Puppeteer and Filmmaker

James Robert Parish

Ferguson
An imprint of Infobase Publishing

Jim Henson: Puppeteer and Filmmaker

Ferguson
An imprint of Infobase Publishing
132 West 31st Street
New York NY 10001

ISBN-10: 0-8160-5834-2
ISBN-13: 978-0-8160-5834-1

Library of Congress Cataloging-in-Publication Data
Parish, James Robert.
    Jim Henson : puppeteer and filmmaker / James Robert Parish.
        p. cm.
    Includes index.
    ISBN 0-8160-5834-2 (hc : alk. paper)
  1. Henson, Jim—Juvenile literature. 2. Puppeteers—United States—Biography—
Juvenile literature. 3. Motion picture producers and directors—United States—
Biography—Juvenile literature. I. Title.
    PN1982.H46P37 2006
    791.5′3092—dc22   200503244

Ferguson books are available at special discounts when purchased in bulk quantitie for businesses, associations, institutions, or sales promotions. Please call our Specia Sales Department in New York at (212) 967-8800 or (800) 322-8755.

You can find Ferguson on the World Wide Web at http://www.fergpubco.com

Text design by David Strelecky

Pages 96–126 adapted from Ferguson's *Encyclopedia of Careers and Vocational Guidan Thirteenth Edition*

Printed in the United States of America

MP FOF 10 9 8 7 6 5 4 3 2

This book is printed on acid-free paper.

CONTENTS

1 A Memorable Creative Contribution   1

2 A Love of Television   8

3 Debut on the Small Screen   21

4 Reaching for Success   35

5 A New TV Horizon   46

6 *Sesame Street* and Beyond   59

7 Fresh Creative Challenges   72

Time Line   90

How to Become a Filmmaker   96

To Learn More about Filmmakers 109

How to Become a Television Director 112

To Learn More about Television
  Directors 124

To Learn More about Jim Henson 127

Index 131

1

A MEMORABLE CREATIVE CONTRIBUTION

In his relatively short life, Jim Henson left an indelible mark on the history of television and the world of show business. In the 1950s and thereafter, his imagination and artistry led to the creation of an enormous number of unique puppets that were perfectly suited for television. Known as the Muppets (Henson's coined word created by combining "marionettes" and "puppets"), these enduring characters—including Kermit the Frog, Miss Piggy, The Great Gonzo, Fozzie Bear, Rowlf the Dog, and countless others—became celebrated across the world.

Several of Henson's beloved Muppets, such as the goofy, oversized Big Bird, the humanoid Ernie, the tiny Elmo, and the ever-hungry Cookie Monster, first came to major viewer attention when showcased as part of the syndicated children's TV program *Sesame Street,* which debuted in 1969 and has been running continuously for more than 35 years. Later, many of these and other delightful Muppets starred in their own internationally syndicated television program, *The Muppet Show* (1976–1981).

Most experts on the history of television rate *Sesame Street* as the most important children's television show ever developed. The chief goal of this groundbreaking children's program is to teach its young viewers a variety of useful topics, including the alphabet and numbers. The show, which is popular both in the United States and around the globe, reaches out to preschoolers from all backgrounds. A key ingredient for the high success of this magical program is Jim Henson's expressive Muppets.

Realizing His Dream

Jim Henson was not content for his imaginative puppet creations to remain solely a part of *Sesame Street.* Rather, he dreamed of finding a proper TV showcase that would focus fully on his adorable, often zany puppets that seem so completely real. He envisioned its humor, satire, and wit to be geared to adults as well as children. With the 1976 debut of *The Muppet Show* Jim realized his ambition. Within two years, at the height of its success, *The Muppet Show* was being syndicated in over 100 countries and watched by more than 235 million people. In the process, the Muppets became the most commercially successful puppets in world history. The show continues to delight new viewers in constant reruns.

Like *Sesame Street, The Muppet Show* won many industry awards, including several Emmy prizes. Over the decades, both of these acclaimed TV shows have been the springboard for a variety of offshoot properties, including theatrical, TV, and direct-to-VHS/DVD feature films and compilations, record albums, books of all types, cartoon strips, touring stage shows and theme park attractions, and a slew of merchandising items ranging from puppets to lunch boxes and to clothing.

A few years ago, when *Time* magazine selected the 100 most influential people of the 20th century in a variety of career categories, its list of major role models included Henson. The publication explained:

> Jim Henson can be credited with many accomplishments: he had the most profound influence on children of any entertainer of his time, he adapted the ancient art of puppetry to the most modern of mediums, television, transforming both; he created a TV show that was one of the most popular on earth. But

Through his imagination and artistry, Jim Henson left an indelible mark on the history of television and the lives of children around the world. (Photofest)

Henson's greatest achievement was broader than any of those. Through his work, he helped sustain the qualities of fancifulness, warmth and consideration that have been so threatened by our coarse, cynical age.

A Man with a Dream

In 1986 Jim Henson, the visionary artist, took time out from his hectic daily schedule to express several of his guiding principles. He said, "I believe that life is basically a process of growth—that we go through many lives choosing those situations and problems that we will learn through. I believe that we form our own lives, that we create our own reality, and that everything works out for the best. I know I drive some people crazy with what seems to be ridiculous optimism, but it has always worked out for me."

He also offered, "At some point in my life I decided, rightly or wrongly, that there are many situations in this life that I can't do much about—acts of terrorism, feelings of nationalistic prejudice, Cold War, etc.—so what I should do is concentrate on the situations that my energy can affect.".

Regarding his choice of media to express his vision, Jim explained, "I believe that we can use television and film to be an influence for good; that we can help to shape the thoughts of children and adults in a positive way. As it has turned out, I'm very proud of some of the work we've done, and I think we can do many more good things."

As for his creative process, Jim said, "I find that it's very important for me to stop every now and then and get recharged and reinspired. The beauty of nature has been one of the great inspirations in my life. Growing up as an artist, I've always been in awe of the incredible beauty of every last bit of design in nature. The wonderful color schemes of nature, which always works harmoniously, are particularly dazzling to me. I love to lie in an open field looking up at the sky. One of my happiest moments of inspiration came to me many years ago as I lay on the grass, looking up into the leaves and branches of a big old tree in California. I remember feeling very much a part of everything and everyone."

Reflecting on his occupation Henson admitted, "Working as I do with the movement of puppet creatures, I'm always struck by the feebleness of our efforts to achieve naturalistic movement. Just looking at the incredible movement of a lizard or a bird, or even the smallest insect, can be a very humbling experience."

Just four years before his untimely passing in May 1990, Henson noted, "When I was young, my ambition was to be one of the people who made a difference in this world. My hope still is to leave the world a little bit better for my having been here. . . . It's a wonderful life and I love it."

Certainly Jim Henson met his noble objectives many times over. He provided generations of audiences with a window into his imaginative world, one filled with profound optimism and a positive sense of wonder. In the process this amazing puppeteer pleased, inspired, and taught lessons about life to people of all ages. He also helped many associates in the field to perfect their craft and to shine in the world of puppetry on their own. As such, Jim Henson created a magnificent legacy.

2

A LOVE OF TELEVISION

James Maury Henson was born on September 24, 1936, at the King's Daughters Hospital in Greenville, Mississippi. Jim was the second son of Paul Ransom Henson and Elizabeth Marcella Henson. Paul was an agronomist (one who studies the science of soil management, land cultivation, and crop production) and worked for the U.S. Department of Agriculture, specializing in researching the development of new strains of forage crops, especially soybeans. Elizabeth was a homemaker.

The Hensons were based in the rural hamlet of Stoneville, Mississippi. The family lived in an old farmhouse in the flat delta lands about a dozen miles from the Mississippi River. While Mrs. Henson focused much of her attention on her shy, bright older boy, Paul Jr., it was Elizabeth's mother, Sarah Brown (known as "Dear"), who devoted the most time to Jimmy (as the boy was called by his family). It was from Dear that Jimmy developed his heightened sense of imagination and optimism. Dear, who loved to read, spent much of her free time making patchwork quilts, painting, and doing knitting and needlework.

Stoneville was a tiny town of about 200 individuals, and there was little to do for amusement there. Jimmy often spent his days wandering around the farmyard. Sometimes, accompanied by his grandmother Dear, he ventured down to the nearby Deer Creek. Early on the boy became fascinated with the sounds and activities of the animals and birds that inhabited the area. As he learned to work with pencil and crayons the youngster began drawing these wondrous creatures that were all around him, often turning these doodles into cartoon sketches. (As a teenager Henson would have one of his cartoons published in the *Christian Science Monitor* newspaper.) He also cut out photos of birds from magazines and added them to the notebooks he kept.

As Jimmy grew a bit older, he accompanied his father and brother—as well as neighbors, including several cousins and uncles—to the local creek for nighttime fishing. Unlike his older brother Paul, who preferred to play with toys such as building blocks, Jimmy chose to draw, using animals and birds for his models. He also began sketching fantastic birds that he dreamed up. Jimmy, the youngest member of the Henson household, also collected turtles and snakes that he dutifully cared for. Already he was dreaming of being tall when he grew up and wanting to do something special with his life. Whereas Paul hoped to follow in his dad's scientific profession, Jimmy's ambitions were more vague. He desired to do something artistic and creative, although he was not yet sure just what that might be.

With both parents usually preoccupied with work, chores, and other priorities and Paul Jr. spending much of the day at elementary school in Leland, Jimmy remained closest to Dear. She would sit with him for hours each day. The two chatted about their mutual love of animals, painting, and the pleasures of simple country life. When young Paul returned from his classroom sessions, often he and his little brother—occasionally accompanied by their cousins—would go swimming at the creek.

Once in a while the boys' father took his two sons to visit the nearby laboratory where he conducted his experiments. It was in this period that one of Mr. Henson's friends, a fellow agriculture researcher, built a tennis court for the Henson boys and other youngsters in the area. Like most local children, the young Hensons enjoyed going to the local movie theater in Leland on Saturday afternoons. One film that made a tremendous impact on young Jimmy was *The Wizard of Oz* (1939). Earlier, Jim had read and loved the series of *Oz* books by L. Frank Baum. Watching this exciting, magical movie led Jimmy to dream of one day creating his own fantasy adventures that would keep audiences— and himself—enthralled.

The New Schoolboy

As his brother Paul Jr. had done, Jimmy began his classroom education at the Leland Grammar School. Although about half of the town's population was African American, the schools were still segregated in the early 1940s, and black youngsters were forced to attend classes in different buildings in Leland.

When Jimmy was in the second grade, the Hensons moved to Hyattsville, Maryland, because Mr. Henson had been reassigned there by the U.S. Department of Agriculture. Living in suburban Hyattsville was quite a contrast to life in rural Mississippi. Sometimes the family drove into Washington, D.C., to tour the nation's capital. Jimmy was particularly impressed with their visit to the Smithsonian Institution as well as their stopover at the Lincoln Memorial to view the immense statue of President Abraham Lincoln.

At their Hyattsville home Jimmy and his family now listened to a radio, and he was excited by his friends' men-tion of television. (TV was then a relatively new form of entertainment. As in the rest of the United States, few people in this Maryland town had TVs.)

Not many months after the Hensons' move to the East, the family returned to Stoneville, Mississippi, when Mr. Henson was again reassigned by his government employers. Soon the boys returned to school in Leland. After school the brothers, who had already experimented with building model planes, trains, and had restored an old organ for Mrs. Henson to play at family sing-alongs, began constructing their own crystal radio set. Jimmy's favorite radio programs at the time included the daring adventures of *The Green Hornet, The Shadow, Red Ryder,* and other action shows.

While Paul Jr. was still gravitating towards the sciences, Jimmy stayed focused on his love of art and began writing poetry. Soon the active youngster had a new activity. He was now old enough to join the Cub Scouts, in which his mother became a local leader.

Every year each scout was required to create a special new project. Wanting to do something different, Jimmy teamed up with his close friend Gordon Jones to come up with a new idea. Young Henson and Jones decided to create a skit in which Gordon would stand in front of the audience with his hands in his pockets. Jimmy would slip his arms around his friend's chest. As Gordon told jokes, Jimmy would smack his pal in the face with a white handkerchief he was waving. Their skit was part of the entertainment put on by the Cub Scouts in the auditorium at the Leland Grammar School and amused their mostly young audience. Jimmy Henson's first effort in show business was a success.

The next year, another den mother for the local Cub Scout chapter encouraged Jimmy to expand upon his stage presentation of the past year. She suggested that he should investigate the use of puppets. This idea appealed to the boy, who was already a great fan of *The Edgar Bergen and Charlie McCarthy Show*, a radio show starring the popular ventriloquist (Bergen) and his array of amusing wooden-headed dummies (e.g., smart-mouthed Charlie McCarthy and dense Mortimer Snerd). Gaining the interest of his friends on the puppet project, it was not long before the boys had their parents buy them basic hand puppets in Greenville. Next, helped by adult relatives, the Cub Scouts constructed a small set for their puppet show. The boys also put together a simple script. In the upcoming talent offering, each member of the den participated with his own puppet. It led to further such puppet shows.

Especially in summertime, the local youngsters spent a lot of time swimming and fishing. They played games

Ventriloquist Edgar Bergen poses with his characters, Charlie McCarthy (left) and Mortimer Snerd (right), in 1938. Bergen's act was an inspiration to the young Henson. (Associated Press)

using rubber-band toy guns. As the children grew older, their fathers taught their sons how to use real guns for hunting. This was an activity Jimmy had absolutely no interest in, however. He much preferred sports such as tennis, roller-skating, or stick hockey (on the tennis courts with the nets taken down), and ice-skating (when the creek froze over in winter).

A Boy with a Special Name

When Jimmy Henson was 11 years old and in the fifth grade, a new boy moved to Leland, Mississippi. His name was T. Kermit Scott. This newcomer and Jimmy became close friends, with young Henson endlessly intrigued by his new pal's unusual middle name. (Neither youngster had any idea at the time that, one day, the name Kermit would become associated with Henson's world-famous frog puppet.)

Henson and his most famous creation, Kermit the Frog (Associated Press)

By now Jimmy had already decided that he wanted a career in the entertainment field. This ambition made him quite different from most of his classmates, who were grounded in more practical thoughts of earning a living in their future. Already far more academically oriented than most of his school chums, Henson also enjoyed putting on shows in his family's spacious back yard. He and Kermit would often borrow sheets from Mrs. Henson's linen shelves to create their costumes—often variations of exotic outfits of the Far East they had read about in books, or seen in magazines and at the movies. Sometimes the boys used the sheets to create tenting to provide shade for their audiences.

When not engrossed in staging these amateur offerings, playing sports, or listening to his favorite radio shows, Jimmy attended to the pony which his parents had bought him and which they kept in the large yard. During the sixth grade Jimmy developed his first school crush—on his classmate Sandra Toler. At the end of that academic year, Mr. Henson told his family that they soon would be moving back to Hyattsville. Maryland, because the U.S. Department of Agriculture had again reassigned him.

Before leaving Stoneville, Jim set free his several frogs, turtles, and snakes, and gave away his mongrel dog

(Toby) because the canine would not be able to run free in the Maryland countryside as he did in Mississippi. The Hensons' pony was sold. After saying goodbye to their friends, the Hensons left for the East, with Stoneville and almost everyone there now part of their past.

A New Beginning

By the fall of 1948 the Hensons were situated in Hyattsville and the boys were attending local schools (with Jimmy in the seventh and Paul Jr. in the ninth grade). More families now owned their own TV sets in their suburban Maryland neighborhood. By now there were about 1 million households in the United States with television sets. It was a growing fad in America for families, friends, and neighbors to crowd around the newly-purchased TV set to watch rather fuzzy (by today's standards) black-and-white images on the small (usually 10-inch) screen. Popular shows at the time on the four existing networks (ABC, CBS, Dumont, and NBC) were *Toast of the Town* (a weekly variety show hosted by syndicated newspaper columnist Ed Sullivan), *Arthur Godfrey's Talent Scouts,* weekly televised exhibitions of wrestling and other sports, and such dramatic series as *Studio One* and *Kraft Television Theater*.

One of the most popular TV offerings was NBC's Tuesday night variety show, *Texaco Star Theater*. By the fall of 1948, club comedian/vaudevillian/movie actor Milton Berle was the permanent master of ceremonies of this program and was gaining enormous popularity throughout the country. Berle, known as "Uncle Miltie," was soon given the nickname "Mr. Television."

The Hensons still did not yet own a TV set. Jimmy, who would have a lifelong fascination with technological gadgets, constantly pestered his family about purchasing one. His parents were not yet convinced such an expense was necessary or would be good for their children (fearing it might distract them too much from their homework). Nevertheless, Jimmy kept begging.

Finally, when Jimmy was 13 and in the seventh grade, the Hensons acquired their own TV set. Years later Henson recalled, "As soon as we got that set, I absolutely loved television. I loved the idea that what you saw was actually taking place at the same time somewhere else."

Very soon the boy had his favorite TV program. It was the NBC network's children show *Kukla, Fran, and Ollie*. The series was a whimsical puppet show created by Burr Tillstrom, based on puppets he had devised back in the mid-1930s. His chief characters were the solemn Kukla (the name is the Russian word for puppet) and the goofy, one-tooth dragon, Oliver "Ollie" J. Dragon. These two simple hand puppets were joined by a live character, Fran Warren, who interacted with the cloth figures. Sometimes the episodes had short musical interludes and long comedy skits. Other times the show presented condensed versions of operettas. On still other occasions the show was devoted to the daily experiences of the rambunctious cast of characters.

In 1950 another new show caught adolescent Jim Henson's imagination. It was CBS-TV's *Life with Snarky Parker,* a children's show featuring the marionette work of Bil Baird and his performer wife, Cora. This simple saga of the Old West was set in Hot Rock. It was produced and directed by actor Yul Brynner and presented a new 15-minute episode each weekday night. Yet another one of Jimmy's TV favorites was the wacky slapstick comedy of mustached, cigar-smoking comedian Ernie Kovacs.

Jim's devotion to TV quickly became stronger than his interest in the Saturday afternoon matinees at the local cinema, listening to radio shows, or reading his favorite newspaper comic strips.

At an age when most adolescents have not seriously made up their minds what career path to follow, Jim

Henson was already set in his choice. Jim intended to fulfill his long-standing dream to be an entertainer and to focus his creative energy in the exciting (and relatively new) field of television.

3

DEBUT ON THE SMALL SCREEN

Once the Henson family had acquired a TV set, Jim quickly became a devoted watcher. Within a few years the teenager was convinced that he wanted, somehow, to work in this new medium. Increasingly impatient at waiting until he had completed his schooling to find employment in his chosen profession, the young man—at the age of 16—began searching for job opportunities within the field. With a confidence well beyond his years, he resourcefully began inquiring at local TV stations (mostly those situated in nearby Washington, D.C.) for any part-time job openings available for a newcomer. His initial efforts met with no success.

Disappointed but undiscouraged, Jim bided his time. Now attending Northwestern High School on Adelphia

Road in Hyattsville, he found a creative outlet by partici-
pating in class plays. Another of his activities was drawing
cover sketches and cartoons for the school's magazine,
Wildcat Scratches. Out of curiosity for the format used by
his puppeteer idols, Henson joined the school's puppet
club. At the time Henson still had no thought of becoming
a professional puppeteer. He just felt it might be fun to
learn more about the field of puppetry, which had been
the road to show business success for television performers whom Jim admired.

The History of Puppetry

As Jim read more about the art of puppetry, he learned
that some of the very earliest types of puppets were ceremonial masks used for tribal rituals thousands of years
old. These masks often had jointed skulls and/or hinged
jaws and were utilized in religious ceremonies. Over
many centuries these masks progressed into simplistic
doll-like figures with moving limbs. Sometimes, as with
the ancient Egyptians, these puppets were made from
terra cotta (a hard, brownish red-fired clay). In North
America, Native American tribes often used puppets for
their ceremonial dances and festivals. Meanwhile, the art
of the puppet theater also developed in ancient Greece.

Also long ago in China, artists began to create shadow
puppets. They were often made from the stretched, dried

skins of sheep, donkeys, water buffaloes, or even fish. Once the translucent (see-through) figures were shaped, they were painted in assorted colors. These figures were placed in front of a screen and light was directed to pass through the images. The multi-hued shadows of the figures could be clearly seen by the audience sitting in front of the screen. As the art further developed, rods or strings were connected to the puppets. By manipulating the rod or strings (one set connected to the figure's neck, and the other to the figure's wrists), these puppets could be made to perform basic actions.

In Turkey, during antiquity, puppeteers created a new variation on shadow puppets. Performers there controlled the puppets from the side of the screen rather than employing the Chinese method of guiding the figures from underneath the screen. The Turks also added waist movements to their shadow puppets. From shadow puppets then developed three-dimensional rod puppets.

Over many centuries, the art of puppetry survived the various historical changes in these countries. The entertainment form was passed on from one generation to another by traveling puppeteers who brought their craft to other lands.

By the Middle Ages, as the Catholic Church became the central institution in Europe, monks and priests were sometimes puppeteers. They used this art form to teach religious doctrine. Thus, Biblical stories such as the birth of Jesus were often presented. In this era marionettes (small, jointed figures operated with strings, and later with wires) became popular for such performances.

As the Middle Ages progressed, many puppeteers expanded beyond strictly religious themes, often adding comic elements. As the Church turned away from the use of puppets to preach, the art of puppetry became increasingly based at local fairs and street gatherings. By the 16th century, puppetry was a popular form of entertainment throughout Europe and some troupes were performing rather sophisticated miniature operas using marionettes.

During the 17th century, a new entertainment fad was the use of hand puppets. These figures had heads and bodies made of soft cloth that would fit over the puppeteer's hand. Because they were far simpler and cheaper to construct, they became increasingly fashionable with puppeteers. By now puppet shows were often performed from small portable stages or, even from the backs of wagons. One popular type of puppet performance was the Punch and Judy show. Their boisterous characters used comedy to discuss topical subjects (especially politics) in an open way that the public at large would never have dared openly debate for fear of reprisal.

By the 20th century in the United States, the art of puppetry led to new variations such as ventriloquism. Ventriloquists produced vocal sounds that seemed to come from the dummy they used in their act. These dummies were often cloth figures with movable limbs and expressive faces (usually made of wood) with movable mouths, eyes, and other features. Among the popular American ventriloquists were such successful entertainers as Edgar Bergen (with dummy Charlie McCarthy) and Paul Winchell (with dummy Jerry Mahoney). Early commercial TV (in the late 1940s) saw the birth of the freckled-faced marionette *Howdy Doody,* as well as the hand puppets in *Kulka, Fran, and Ollie,* the offerings of Bil and Cora Baird, as well as Shari Lewis and her lovable, baby-talking Lambchop.

A Lucky Break

In 1954, just after he graduated from Northwestern High School, 17-year-old Jim Henson got his chance to perform on TV. A local area (CBS network) TV station, WTOP, was in need of puppeteers for its Saturday morning program, *Junior Good Morning Show.* Because the station's budget was too limited to hire professionals, it turned to students to find low-cost performers who would work for $10 a day.

WTOP sent two production assistants to Jim's high school to solicit interest in the job opening from members of Northwestern's puppet club.

Now a tall, gangling fellow at six feet, three inches, Jim applied for the position. He turned to a classmate, Russell Wall, to help with the upcoming audition. Together, they whipped up several crude hand puppets (operated with three fingers of a hand), including Pierre the French Rat, as well as two cowboy characters they named Longhorn and Shorthorn. (Throughout his career, Henson used puppet duos with contrasting shapes and characters.) The two enthusiastic young men did their run-through at WTOP and were hired. Unfortunately, the new weekend TV show only lasted a few weeks before being cancelled.

However, Henson and Wall's puppet performances had been well reviewed by local newspapers. Jim used these favorable critiques as part of his resume kit when he made the rounds of other Washington, D.C., TV stations seeking employment. Management at WRC-TV, an NBC network owned-and-operated station, was impressed by Henson's credentials and obvious creativity. He was hired to work on some of the outlet's local programming.

Parental Concern

Jim's father, a devoted scientist, was becoming increasingly concerned about his younger son's passionate interest in the seemingly frivolous new world of TV and the art of puppetry (which Paul Sr. felt was child's play). His father repeatedly explained to Jim that show business was a shaky way of earning a livelihood. He insisted that the young man would have a much more secure financial future working in the field of science. The more his dad kept insisting that Jim should be more like his older brother, Paul Jr. (i.e., take a real interest in science courses and perhaps become an engineer), the more the young man remained determined to pursue his own future.

In the fall of 1954, Jim entered the University of Maryland located in College Park, about three miles from the Hensons' home. Trying to be more agreeable to his father's vision of what his work future should encompass, the entering freshman unenthusiastically took a few science classes. He soon realized that he had no aptitude— let alone interest—for such studies. He switched to a major in commercial art/theater arts, thinking he might become a commercial artist if his dreams of working full time in television did not come to be.

Several of Jim's drawings from his early college years survive and reveal the student to have a lively imagination, a knack for colors, and a skill for creating elaborate fantasy scenes. These works display a surprising amount of intriguing detail created with relatively few strokes. In retrospect, one can see the relationship between such creative efforts (which also included cartoons) and Henson's later hand puppets, which were remarkably simple but captivating and expressive.

During the time Jim was studying at the University of Maryland he had to enroll in the home economics department in order to earn his degree in commercial art. In that era "home ec" (as it was called) was largely the province of female students whose post-college plans consisted of getting married, running a household, and raising a family. When Henson told people he was a home ec major—one of the few men on campus to have such a course of study—he was amused by the surprised reactions he received.

Unmindful of other people's attitudes, Jim took as many art and theater arts courses as possible. One of his classes was in puppetry, a subject taken by most students (usually seniors) as a lark, believing it was an easy way to gain academic credits. By now, Jim knew from experience that puppeteering could be a useful way to earn money and perhaps to get ahead in TV, and he took his puppet class very seriously. Always ambitious and enthusiastic about whatever he tackled, he took the initiative of devising puppet shows for he and his classmates to perform and did a great deal to bolster the other students' interest in their study of puppetry.

TV Studio Work

At WRC-TV, Jim worked part time on the station weekday show *Afternoon*. It was a magazine-style program aimed at housewives. As part of this program, he had a five-minute showcase performing a puppet show in a regular feature entitled "Inga's Angle." Needing a new helper for this on-air project, he turned to Jane Nebel, a classmate from New York who was an art major at the University of Maryland. She and Jim met in the puppet class they both took on campus. It was not too long before Jim and Jane began dating.

As Henson performed his "Inga's Angle" show, he found the work emotionally liberating. Now nearing 19, the tall young man, who hid his acne behind a bushy beard, was usually quite shy in public. However, when he was performing goofy antics with his hand puppets he could express the witty, offbeat thoughts he typically kept bottled within himself. ("Puppets," Henson once said, "are fortunate—they can do and say things a live performer wouldn't touch with a stick.") The experience was invigorating for Jim and he began to take the craft of puppeteering even more seriously.

When Jim was not performing his short, daily TV segment, he hung around the studio, often in the control room. He was fascinated by the various elements that went into making a television show and how the technicians pulled all the pieces together for airing. When it would not interfere with their studio work, Henson asked many questions of the cameramen and other employees. In the process, the inquisitive young man learned a great deal about the still-primitive medium of TV, especially how the TV cameras (with their variety of lens) worked and what lighting schemes were most effective. At the same time his new studio friends did their best to guide Jim through practical steps to make his daily TV work as professional as possible.

In May of 1955, WRC-TV management showed their appreciation for their new employee by offering the young man his own TV show. In actuality it was two short (five-minute) spots, but in key time slots. He was assigned to 6:25 P.M. (right before the much-watched new program *The Huntley-Brinkley Report*) and at 11:25 P.M. (just after the late evening news and just before NBC network's *Tonight* show with Steve Allen). In this lineup Henson's dual showcase would be seen by a great number of WRC-TV's viewership.

Jim's puppet program, which debuted on May 9, 1955, was called *Sam and Friends.* It featured a manic character called Sam, a humorous-looking hand puppet who boasted a bald dome, big eyes, protruding ears, and a round funny nose. Other characters on the groundbreaking entry were even more bizarre, all springing from Jim's fertile imagination. They included Yorick, a talking skull with a hearty appetite for anything in sight. Another of Henson's stock company of figures was Kermit (named after his childhood pal), the first version of what would become the famous Muppet frog. In constructing Kermit, Jim scrounged at home through his mother's rag bag. He found some green material from one of her old coats, and sewed together a hand puppet. To make the figure's eyes he cut ping-pong balls in half. He glued them to the "face" and painted representations of eyes.

In its debut version Kermit (who often wore a silly wig) really did not greatly resemble the later Kermit the Frog of *The Muppet Show* fame. According to Jim, "He was much more lizardlike." He noted, "People would say, 'Oh, you've got a frog,' and I'd say, 'No, it's just a creature.'"

Love and Work

At the time Jim was offered his *Sam and Friends* gig at the Washington, D.C., TV station, Jane Nebel was then completing her senior year at the university and planning on a teaching career. Henson asked his girlfriend to continue working with him on the new program, to which Jane agreed. Even before Jim was fully aware of it, she sensed that their futures were to be intertwined.

Although Henson was still a relative beginner in show business and a newcomer in the TV field, he had already made astute decisions about the use of puppets on the small screen. He believed that because the medium was such an intimate one with the viewer relatively close to the TV screen, traditional methods of presenting puppet shows should be discarded. Rather than have his puppets perform on a box-like tiny stage that framed the action in a small space, he created his set as a much larger space in

In shows such as this one (Muppet Classic Theater, Three Little Pigs), Jim had his puppets perform in broad sets with many camera close-ups. This made the shows more like regular, live-action television programs than traditional puppet shows. (Photofest)

which the puppets would operate with the close-up cameras directed fully at the puppets' set. It gave the setting a much broader look, similar to watching a live-action show with real-life characters.

To perform with his puppets, Jim would compact his tall frame behind the high stage "wall" where the puppets sat and interacted, allowing the figures to have a far greater range of activity than was the custom. (One of Henson's other innovations was to provide himself and the other puppeteers with TV monitors placed on the floor near to where they were crouching. This way they had a "view" of what was going on in front of the camera and could gauge their hand movements/puppets accordingly. The difficulty in using monitors was that they showed the action in reverse: i.e., when a figure appeared to move to the right on the screen, in actuality it was moving to the left.)

Breaking from the standard practice of using hand puppets with little mobility to their faces, Jim realized that by creating a striking suggestion of facial features on soft flexible material (which later included using foam rubber) he had far greater options. He discovered that with sufficient practice he could create the suggestion for viewers that these puppet figures had animated faces that registered a wide range of emotions and reactions. Because this NBC network station was an early color TV broadcaster, Jim got experience in combining vivid hues in his figures and settings to grab his viewers' attention.

Jim's insights into how to adapt puppetry for the special demands of TV were the breakthroughs that would set him on the path to tremendous career success.

4

REACHING FOR SUCCESS

A typical episode of *Sam and Friends* involved Kermit sitting on a wall while interacting with one or more of the other creatures (such as Mushmellon, Moldy Hay, bushy-haired Professor Madcliffe, sinister Icky Gunk, and big-mouthed Hank). Kermit's prime opponent was the dastardly Yorick, who always had his greedy eyes set on gobbling up anything in sight, including the green-skinned Kermit. During the five-minute segment manned by Jim Henson (especially as Kermit) and girlfriend Jane Nebel (especially as Yorick), Kermit and the other featured characters would lip-synch to a popular song. Meanwhile, the other hyperactive onstage figures would keep up the action, no matter how silly.

In the initial five-minute *Sam and Friends* segments neither Jim nor Jane would speak any dialogue for their characters. (Later, as Jim adventurously developed more complex skits for his showcase, he and Jane used their voices.) Usually the brief interlude would end with a quick dramatic action, such as Yorick firmly grabbing Kermit's leg with his mouth, dragging the latter off-camera to an unknown fate. (Henson once said of these segments, "In the early days of the Muppets we had two endings. Either one creature ate the other or both of them blew up. So I've always been particular to things eating other things.")

Aired twice daily, *Sam and Friends* quickly used up material, so Jim was always imagining new ideas for skits. Henson was lucky because TV was then still so relatively new that there were few rules to be broken. And in a larger sense, the 1950s was an era of new creative trends, including the expansion of jazz music, the rise of rock-and-roll, and a growing rebellion against the conservatism and conformity of the era.

With this atmosphere of creative experimentation in the air, Jim felt more inclined to try anything that came to mind on *Sam and Friends*. He believed that because the twice-daily show was such a short program, no one in authority probably was paying much attention to the far-out proceedings he was providing and, thus, he could let his vivid imagination run wild. (He proved to be correct because, as he observed later, "There was never a complaint or any attempt at censorship of any kind.")

Thus, his Muppets (as he had named his array of strange-looking creatures) got into many unusual on-camera situations and interactions. They were based on Jim's delightfully wacky point of view, in which the unanticipated became normal. By carefully choosing music to underscore the characters' zany and unpredictable activities, Jim created fun miniature TV segments.

Besides his scriptwriting and performing, Henson built his odd hand puppets, constructed the sets and props, and created unique opening credits for the shows that veered far from the standard, formal title cards used for most TV offerings of the time.

The Entrepreneur

While Jim was involved with *Sam and Friends* he was a full-time student at the University of Maryland. A bright and intellectual student, he devoted the necessary time and effort to keep up with all of his class work, while pursuing his various extracurricular activities. His interests, besides the TV industry, painting and drawing cartoons, and puppet work, included a fascination with jazz. He would often visit local clubs to hear jazz musicians perform.

While Jim's TV job helped to pay for his college tuition, he undertook additional and much-needed money-making activities, which proved to tie into his ambition of becoming a commercial artist. Thus, Jim set up a silk-screen poster business. Soon he had a thriving operation making signs, banners, and so forth for an array of local customers. As time passed, Henson had enough extra money to buy himself a fancy used car—a Rolls Royce Silver Cloud—that he would drive to his college graduation. With this flashy vehicle he felt he had really arrived in life.

In the midst of multi-talented Jim's growing success, he and his family suffered a great tragedy. Henson's gentle-natured brother, Paul, then 22 and engaged to be married, was killed in a car accident in April 1956. The calamity strongly affected everyone in the Henson household. Jim and his older brother had always been close, and losing Paul Jr. was an especially difficult emotional hurdle for Jim to overcome. Many close to the Jim thought that the death marked Henson for life. Thereafter, Jim seemed to work at an even faster speed, more determined than ever to accomplish a great deal in his life before it might be suddenly snuffed out.

Gaining Recognition

In the same year that Jim lost his brother Paul, he received a great career boost. He and Jane were invited to perform a *Sam and Friends* skit on Steve Allen's NBC network talk program, *Tonight*. Their appearance was a big success and created great word-of-mouth for the puppet performers. It led to TV guest appearances on other variety/talk programs.

During 1957, the already busy Henson added to his profitable activities. The growing popularity of *Sam and Friends* and the antic, anti-establishment humor of the Muppets led Wilkins Coffee to ask Jim to use his hand puppets to create commercials for the company. Serving as writer, director,

Jim and his creations for Sam and Friends *(Photofest)*

and performer, Henson came up with an 8-second coffee ad that caught his client's fancy. As Jim explained, "Till then the agencies believed that the hard sell was the only way to get their message over on television. We took a very different approach. We tried to sell things by making people laugh."

In these brief commercials Jim actually spoke dialogue on camera as he and Jane, who remained a silent puppeteer, performed little vignettes that in one wacky way or another pitched Wilkins Coffee to viewers. The initial ads—featuring the puppets Wilkins (who adored coffee) and Wontkins (who repeatedly refused to try the beverage)—were so successful that Wilkins Coffee remained a contented client through well over 200 spot ads.

As time progressed and Jim's success as a unique pitchman became known throughout the television industry, he added an impressive number of important clients, including Ivory Snow, Royal Crown Cola, IBM, Wilson's Certified Bacon, Gleem toothpaste, and Purina Dog Chow. Not only were these assignments lucrative, but they inspired Henson to develop a virtual stock company of Muppet characters to perform in offbeat, attention-grabbing TV ads.

Often these new additions to the stable of Muppets would develop into more refined versions used in later projects. For example, Rowlf the Dog emerged for the Purina Dog Chow ads and, later, turned up when Henson was on TV's *The Jimmy Dean Show* (1963–1966). Another character was made for a commercial campaign for La Choy canned Chinese food. Henson put together his first full-size Muppet, the La Choy Dragon. This impressively huge character, which had a person enclosed inside the figure to operate its movement, was the springboard for the celebrated Big Bird on *Sesame Street*, a character which had its direct genesis in commercials created for Stouffer's Frozen Foods.

Sometimes the new Muppets paved the way for other advancements. For example, color TV was just starting to become popular as the cost of color sets was coming down and the average consumer could now consider purchasing one. The La Choy Dragon, which has a multi-colored patchwork of skin colors, spit forth a fiery breath that was accomplished with smoke of various hues. This innovation looked very effective on color TV. This work required Jim to develop a palette of colors that would grab viewers' imagination as the age of color television dawned.

In addition, unlike the similar broadcasts of *Sam and Friends,* the commercials Jim produced were filmed so they could be more elaborate and repeated often. In the process of writing, directing, producing, and acting in these productions, Henson learned a great deal about the allied medium of film.

As in later years, Jim was constantly fascinated with experimenting and discovering new methods to improve the presentation of the Muppets. In the process he would plow back a good portion of his profits into research (whether on his own part, or that of his growing staff).

With his various money-earning activities becoming increasingly successful, Jim formalized his operations into a professional business. In the process he and Jane legally became business partners. In 1958, his operation was incorporated as Muppets Inc.

Europe-Bound

By the time Jim graduated from the University of Maryland in 1958, he was a successful businessman with a college degree. Jim had developed a new attitude regarding his puppetry work. He admitted, "All the time I was in school I didn't take puppetry seriously. I mean, it didn't seem to be the sort of thing a grown man works at for a living." But no longer was his puppet work a child's hobby, or merely something to amuse himself and to help support his way through college. Puppetry was a creative craft that had brought him significant recognition from his peers. In the process, the work allowed him the opportunity to use the full of range of his creativity to lead the art form to new heights in the growing arena of television.

Thus, Jim decided to study the origins of his profession further. This meant taking a trip to Europe to research the subject and, in the process, to meet renowned puppeteers.

With the money Henson was accumulating from his assorted commercial enterprises, he could afford the journey abroad. However, he had to solve the problem of what to do about the ongoing *Sam and Friends* show. WCR-TV did not want the increasingly successful, attention-grabbing *Sam and Friends* to end its popular run. Thus, to accommodate Jim's trip overseas they agreed for Jane Nebel to be temporarily teamed on-camera with Henson's old school pal, Bob Payne.

Once abroad, Jim discovered that people in Europe had a far different attitude about puppetry. Unlike Americans, who generally thought such work was fit only as diversion for children, in Europe the puppetry art (which focused on the telling of traditional fairy/folk tales) was held in high regard. Talking with fellow craftspeople, he discovered, "They were very serious about their work." As he explored the field more thoroughly he saw how puppets could be a high art form in which the figures were carefully crafted and remarkable to behold. While attending puppet shows in various European cities he noted that the audiences were not just composed largely of youngsters, but also included individuals of all ages.

Returning to the United States, Jim's enthusiasm for his puppet work increased. ("I came back from that trip all fired up to do wonderful puppetry.") This highly charged positive attitude was reinforced when *Sam and Friends* won a local Emmy Award in 1958 for Best Local Entertainment Program. Flattered by the industry recognition, 21-year-old Jim felt he was truly on the right path for his future. He shared his joy with his partner Jane Nebel. Together they returned to performing on *Sam and Friends* and doing their various TV ads.

One ambitious project that sprang from Jim's trip abroad was an elaborate retelling of *Hansel and Gretel*. Despite several efforts, the overly complicated, formal production—geared in the European classic tradition—never gelled properly and was eventually abandoned. From such failures, Jim learned a great deal of what worked and where he should aim his efforts.

Getting Married

By now Jim and Jane had known each other for over four years. During this time they had participated in a successful TV show and established an allied business enterprise. Between working so much together and dating, they had developed an extremely close bond. The duo decided it was time to marry. (As a wedding gift for his wife-to-be, Jim agreed to his mother's nagging that he shave off his beard. He sent the clipped hair to Jane accompanied by a note which read, "From Samson to Delilah.") They wed in a traditional ceremony—with the nonconformist groom even wearing a suit—on May 28, 1959. They purchased a home in nearby Bethesda, Maryland, converting their basement into a convenient workshop for creating and repairing their *Sam and*

Friends puppets. Within a year, the couple became parents of their first child, Lisa.

Having started a family, the young couple was eager to see how they would fare in the world of puppetry in the new decade.

5

A NEW TV
HORIZON

In 1960, the increasingly popular Muppets made their debut appearance on NBC-TV's *Today* show. Jim, always experimenting and reaching out for new avenues to showcase his puppets, did drawings for an unpublished children's book, which centered on the adventures of Kermit, Yorick, and an intriguing stash of watermelon seeds. Also that same year, Jim and Jane Henson, along with eight-week old Lisa, drove to Detroit, Michigan, to attend the annual Puppeteers of America convention. In the Motor City, Jim met some of his idols, including Burr Tillstrom. As a fun caper, Henson and Tillstrom drove into midtown in Jim's Rolls Royce. There, with the car parked, Jim put on an impromptu puppet performance, featuring Kermit, through the sunroof.

The next year, when the Puppeteers of America held their convention in Anaheim, California, the Hensons attended the festivities. Jane was expecting another baby (daughter Cheryl) and had decided to retire from active performance with the Muppets and become a full-time housewife and mother. Therefore, Jim needed to find a replacement for the invaluable contributions that his wife made in their puppet activities.

At the Anaheim convention, Jim was introduced to the 17-year old Frank Oznowicz, son of Mike and Frances Oznowicz, who were acclaimed puppeteers themselves. Frank was very intrigued with the world of puppetry and was already a whiz with the art form. He quickly impressed Henson with his knowledge of, and enthusiasm for, the craft. However, he still had high school to complete and could not accept Jim's offer to become part of the Muppets team.

Still needing a new team player, Jim turned to Jerry Juhl, another attendee at the Puppeteers' gathering. Juhl was an experienced children's TV show performer who had been working at a San Jose, California, station. Years later, Juhl recalled the casual meeting he had with Henson in the parking lot outside the convention building. Jerry remembers Jim grabbing a black box from the trunk of his car. "The things he brought out of that box seemed to me to be magical presences, like totems—but funnier: an angry creature whose whole body was a rounded triangle; a purple skull named Yorick; a green froglike thing. One

Frank Oz (Oznowicz) was Jim's friend and collaborator for much of his career. (Landov)

after another, Jim pulled them from the box, put them on his hand, and brought them to life. . . . this guy was like a sailor who had studied the compass and found that there was a fifth direction in which one could sail. When he offered me a berth on that ship, I signed on." Now part of the Henson team, Jerry would take over for Jane in performing Muppet routines for *Sam and Friends*; later he would become a key part of the squad as head writer on *The Muppet Show* and other entertainment ventures.

Another soon-to-be hired member of the growing Henson squad was Don Sahlin, who had been a stop-motion animator on *The Time Machine* (1960) and other movies. He had also worked with Burr Tillstrom on *Kukla, Fran & Ollie*. The fun-loving, prankish Sahlin became the organization's primary designer and builder of characters.

Henson once recalled his work with playful Sahlin (who, in his spare time, delighted in creating oddball contraptions for the Henson workplace): "The way Don and I used to work, I would generally do a little scribble on a scrap of paper—which Don would regard with a certain reverence as being the 'essence' which he was working toward. The work was a pleasant cooperative effort during which we would talk about the character and often change it quite a bit . . . . Don had a very simple way of working—reducing all nonessential things and homing in on what was important. . . . [Sahlin] had more to do with the basic style than people think of as 'the Muppets' than anybody else."

Moving to New York

In 1961, now the parent of two children and with his wife Jane retired from the craft, Jim Henson decided to end the long-time run of *Sam and Friends*. It is likely that the successful series could have continued for several more years. However, Jim wanted to expand his experience in the TV field and did not want to be limited by his now syndicated TV series. Signing Bernie Brillstein as talent agent to promote the Muppets, Jim leaped into new projects.

While continuing the Muppets' frequent appearances on NBC's *Today* show, Jim was involved in the making of a TV series pilot. The unsold sitcom was called *Mad, Mad World.* Another project was *Tales of the Tinkerdee,* an intricate fairy-tale puppet program filled with one-line jokes and sight gags. This ambitious project never aired, however.

By 1962, the Hensons were living in Manhattan in the same upscale apartment building where Burr Tillstrom resided. Jim set up his puppet shop in a brownstone building on East 53rd Street. (The headquarters consisted of two upstairs rooms and a bathroom.) The staff included Jim, Jerry Juhl, Don Sahlin, and, in August 1963, expanded to include Frank Oznowicz. Frank, who soon adopted the professional surname of Oz, had graduated from high school and was undecided about pursuing a college education.

Recalling the initial Muppets studio in New York City, Frank Oz described, "Don Sahlin worked in the back workshop next to Jim's animation stand and opposite the big Yorick head. . . . Jerry Juhl had a desk in the front room. . . . Opposite Jerry's desk there was a dartboard on the closet door with lots and lots of holes on the door.

Jim poses with some of the earliest versions of the Muppets.
(Photofest)

Above the dartboard hung the papier-mâché moose head that would light up. There was a big black chair and ottoman. Jim's chair. He would sit on it or lie in it, working on character or script ideas."

Jumping Ahead

It was Don Sahlin whom Jim assigned to create Rowlf the Dog (and his sidekick Baskerville) for the company's new client, Purina Dog Chow. One of Don's biggest contributions to the growth of the Muppets was to simplify the look of the puppets while enhancing the figures' expressive range.

Rowlf became so popular on Purina TV commercials that in the fall of 1963 the character became a prime figure of *The Jimmy Dean Show*, a 60-minute musical variety show from ABC-TV. A highlight of the weekly show was country singer Dean's exchanges and duets with the Muppet hound, the piano-playing Rowlf (whom the star called "my ol' buddy"). The puppet—famous for his double takes and witticisms—was operated by Henson with Frank Oz's help, while Jim provided the dog's voice. The well-received seven-to-eight-minute segments featuring Dean and Rowlf were a regular feature of the program.

Working on *The Jimmy Dean Show* (which lasted until April 1966) was a tremendous learning opportunity for Jim Henson. This was also true when Jimmy Dean headlined in Las Vegas and Rowlf the Dog was part of the act. Performing in front of a live audience was a new and useful experience for Henson.

Whereas on *Sam and Friends,* the short comic skits were often spontaneous, *The Jimmy Dean Show* had a carefully developed script in which, for the first time, his puppet was interacting with a live talent. (Jim, who thrived on wearing vivid, flower-print ties, was still a shy man in public who talked in a voice barely above a whisper, and whose favorite comment was variations of "Mmmmm," or "It will be okay.")

Jim pointed out, "Jimmy Dean was great from a point of view of learning the craft, and Rowlf was the first, solid, fully rounded personality we did."

During this period in which sons Brian (1963) and John (1965) were born, the Hensons moved their growing family to Greenwich, Connecticut, where they bought a home. Its walls and some of their furniture soon became decorated with doodlings, drawings, and designs created by the entire Henson household. The Muppets center of operation remained in the modest office in Manhattan.

The Novice Filmmaker

Jim Henson had long been excited by the potentials of moviemaking. He had experimented with this medium a bit with his TV commercials, which were shot on film.

Jim's earlier experiences in film, in the late 1950s, used a 16-mm Bolex camera and an animation stand to make his college artwork "move." He said, "I started painting on a sheet of paper placed under the lens on the bed of the animation stand. I would just paint a couple of strokes and take a frame or two of film, and I would be able to watch this painting evolve and move. From that time on I lost interest in . . . straight painting as such because the aspect of movement in animation was so much more fascinating."

By 1964, with his career in high gear, Jim still found time to experiment. Jim recalled keeping a balance between his professional and personal creative efforts at this time, saying, "I used to think in terms of having two careers going—two threads that I was working on at the same time. One was accepted by the audience and was successful, and that was the Muppets. The other was something I was very interested in and enjoyed very much, but it didn't have any commercial success—which didn't bother me because I got so much pleasure from working on those noncommercial projects."

Because he was "interested in the visual image and all [the] different ways of using it," in 1964 he began work on *Time Piece*, a nine-minute short subject. It was a tale of an individual trapped by time (and deadlines and routines). The experimental picture involved the use of time in other disciplines: music, philosophy, and so forth. It involved a depressed character (played by Jim) who is confined to a hospital bed. He escapes and undergoes several adventures that are tied together by the film's pulsating soundtrack. Lurching across space and time, the fast-moving and jump-cut filled narrative was an ancestor of music videos, which would follow 20 years later.

Whenever Henson and his staff could spare any precious time from their paying activities, they worked on bits and pieces of *Time Piece*. For this venture, Jim was director, producer, primary scripter, actor, and stuntperson. He also pulled everyone he knew into service, whether it be family, friends, or staff.

Describing this side project, Jim said, "I was playing with a flow-of-consciousness form of editing, where one image took you to another image and there was no logic to it but your mind put it together. . . . I've always felt that the visual image is very powerful—music and image together, I guess. Those two things work on one level for me, while the spoken word and dialogue work at a much shallower level."

Time Piece premiered at the Museum of Modern Art in May 1965. Thereafter it played a lengthy run at a Manhattan movie theater. *Time Piece* was eventually nominated for an Academy Award in the Best Short Subject category, though it lost out to another film.

Excited by his artistic and commercial success with *Time Piece,* Jim went on to make two other short subjects. Both of these aired on TV, as part of the NBC network's *Experiments in Television* series. One was entitled *Youth '68* and focused on young Americans in the 1960s Summer of Love era. This program aired in spring 1968.

In 1969 Henson did *The Cube,* which took three years to make. Written with Jerry Juhl and featuring actor Richard Schaal, this abstract film deals with a man imprisoned for some unexplained reason in a stark white room. His mysterious confinement is constantly inter-rupted by characters who, unlike him, have the ability to enter/leave the room. The surreal film aired on NBC-TV in 1969. During this time Jim also started work on *Cyclia,* an elaborate, three-dimensional mix of visuals and sound effects that he planned to showcase in a nightclub. Although *Cyclia* was never completed, it was just another example of Jim's multifaceted creativity during this period.

Growing Fame for the Muppets

While Jim and his crew were working on their experi-mental film projects, the Henson organization continued to have high visibility. On September 18, 1966, Jim and the Muppets made the first of many appearances on the top-rated TV variety hour, *The Ed Sullivan Show.* This weekly showcase for talent was an important stepping stone for the Muppets, for *The Ed Sullivan Show* had a large and devoted audience all across the nation.

The Muppets made appearances on other TV series and specials. Rowlf the Dog also hosted *Our Place,* a CBS network summer series in 1967. In addition, the much in-demand Rowlf became the spokesperson for a series of IBM films used for in-house training conferences.

During this active phase, Jim kept hoping he could convince a network to give the Muppets their own show. However, executives still believed that the amusing puppets were just a novelty that could not sustain an ongoing series. It was their opinion that Henson's characters would not appeal to a sufficiently large crowd of adults. This constant rejection of a Muppets TV program frustrated the usually optimistic Jim Henson. His wife, Jane, remembered, "Jim began to feel maybe he should be looking in another direction."

Meanwhile, Henson and his crew became involved with writers/producers Jon Stone and Tom Whedon, who had sold a concept for a TV pilot to ABC-TV. The concept was to retell the Cinderella fairytale over several months with all sorts of live action and puppet figures involved. The pilot was shot in October 1965, but was not aired or further developed. In 1968, the team of Stone-Whedon-Henson expanded the idea into a 60-minute special entitled *Hey, Cinderella!* That intricate production eventually was aired by ABC-TV in 1970.

The Cinderella project led to two other similar Henson efforts: *The Frog Prince* and *The Muppet Musicians of Bremen*. *The Frog Prince* featured Kermit, now fully identifiable as a frog (complete with flippers). *The Muppet Musicians of Bremen,* which was set in the Louisiana bayous, featured several barnyard animals with an amazing aptitude for playing Dixieland music. These two shows, under the umbrella title of *Tales from Muppetland,* aired in 1972 and featured such new members of the Henson puppeteer staff as Richard Hunt, John Lovelady, and Jerry Nelson.

A Golden Opportunity

During this fruitful period of the late 1960s, the next chapter in the Jim Henson story would develop, as he became involved with the groundbreaking new children's TV series, *Sesame Street*.

6

SESAME STREET AND BEYOND

In 1966 the well-regarded Carnegie Institute inaugurated a research study devoted to children's television. It was their belief that television could be used as a tool to instruct young viewers, especially underprivileged young-sters in inner cities. Joan Ganz Cooney, who produced documentaries and news specials for WNET (the public television channel in New York City), took a leave of absence from her post to head this milestone project as its executive director.

Cooney and her staff learned that most children's pro-gramming on American television at the time was nearly empty of educational content and talked down to chil-dren. They concluded that such programming was little more than a pacifier for young audiences. To correct this situation, Cooney suggested that public television could broadcast useful programming for young viewers. This, in turn, led to a large fund-raising drive and the establishment of the Children's Television Workshop (CTW). By 1968, CTW was gathering a staff whose first priority was to put together a TV show aimed at preschoolers. Funding was supplied by, among others, the U.S. Office of Information, the Carnegie Corporation, the Ford Foundation, the Markle Foundation, and Operation HeadStart.

Among those hired for the CTW project was Jon Stone, who, along with Dave Connell and Sam Gibbon, would be producers on the new public television series. One of the things this team decided was that their upcoming show should—in one way or another—include puppets. Stone, who had worked with Henson and the Muppets on the *Hey, Cinderella!* show, brought up Jim and his lively hand puppets as likely candidates for the show. Cooney knew the Muppets from their popular TV commercials and from a 1968 PBS-TV special (*Muppets on Puppets*) but had not thought about using them. When she first met Henson she was apprehensive about working with the tall, gangly, bearded man whose typical wardrobe was a T-shirt, jeans, and loafers. However, after talking with Jim and getting to know this gentle, creative, and whimsical man, she realized he would be a good fit for CTW.

At first, Jim had reservations about becoming involved with this planned children's small-screen show. He wanted to focus on adult TV programming and continue his work with experimental filmmaking and TV commercials.

Several factors persuaded Jim to change his mind about joining CTW. For one thing, the recent, tragic assassinations of presidential candidate Robert Kennedy and civil rights leader Martin Luther King Jr. had contributed a new atmosphere of social consciousness in the United States. It was time where progressive individuals such as Henson wanted to help change the course of the nation's society, economy, and civil rights. Jane Henson said of her late husband's decision to work with CTW, "Jim agreed to do *Sesame Street* because it gave him the opportunity to work on a wide variety of things—puppetry, animation— and also because of our children. It was through them that he had begun to realize that children could be a very sophisticated audience."

Launching the New TV Series

Having linked up with CTW, Jim enthusiastically collaborated with the show's producers and Joe Raposo (the musical director) to formulate the program's format. The pilot was shot in July 1969 and given the name *Sesame Street* (a play on the folk tale command "Open Sesame!").

The innovative show was set on a city street so that inner-city preschoolers, in particular, would relate to its locale. Taking advantage of young people's attraction to TV commercials with their snappy editing and catchy jingles, *Sesame Street* used a mix of puppetry, animation, and live actors to present informative skits and songs. Through its very entertaining design, *Sesame Street* taught young viewers about the alphabet, numbers, grammatical concepts, health issues, social concerns, and so forth.

Sesame Street was written so that viewers of various age levels could learn something from and enjoy the show. The *Sesame Street* neighborhood featured actors of various ethnic backgrounds, bolstered by an array of bizarre and captivating puppet characters.

The show debuted on November 10, 1969, on more than 170 stations of the National Education Television network. It met with great enthusiasm. *Daily Variety* reported, "The only thing wrong with *Sesame Street* is that it took 20 years to get here. Otherwise it's a noble effort in a noble cause and well financed. . . . Most important, it's also well done."

Initially the show was funded for a 29-week season. It quickly smoothed out its formula and its mix of live action, animation (much of which was produced by Jim Henson), and the antics of the Muppets. While the human performers such as Will Lee (playing Mr.

Hooper), Bob McGrath (as Bob), Loretta Long (as Susan), and Matt Robinson (as Gordon), it was Jim Henson's unique Muppet characters such as Big Bird, Bert and Ernie, Cookie Monster, and Oscar the Grouch that really impressed viewers. Jane Henson provided the movements for assorted Muppets, but after the birth of their fifth child, Heather, she pretty much dropped out of participation.

With *Sesame Street* a great success, there was no question that the show would return for future seasons. As the pace accelerated to create new Muppets to join the existing inhabitants of *Sesame Street,* Henson's staff expanded. Meanwhile, the Henson organization had given up doing TV commercials for the time being, feeling it would be inappropriate during their early involvement with the public-spirited *Sesame Street.*

Capitalizing on Success

As *Sesame Street* became an established hit, the Henson organization had to move to a bigger space in Manhattan to keep up with the demands of producing new figures (as well as refurbishing previously introduced characters), creating special effects, and turning out the animated segments of the show. Jim was kept constantly busy supervising his growing staff and fulfilling the demands of his contributions to the ongoing program.

The cast of Sesame Street, *the most successful and longest-running children's program on television.* (Photofest)

In 1970, the year that Big Bird appeared on the cover of prestigious *Time* magazine, the first *Sesame Street* record album was released. The merchandising of characters from this show snowballed and, in short order, the entire world seemed to know *Sesame Street*. (As one Henson associate described the show's success, "*Sesame Street* is an extraordinary story about how an experiment just took off and became part of the very fabric of our culture.") Soon syndicated around the globe, the dubbed and/or subtitled show often had inserted segments tailored to the country in which it was being aired.

As *Sesame Street* continued on its successful path, winning many industry awards in the process, it proved to be a wonderful showcase for the Muppets. It prompted a great demand for Jim Henson's creations to appear on a variety of TV shows/specials. When Frank Sinatra's daughter, Nancy, a singer/actor, headlined a Las Vegas casino club act in 1971, she hired a contingent of Muppets to be part of her stage show. In 1973, the Muppets were featured in ABC-TV's *The Muppets Valentine Special*. Miss Piggy, one of the most popular Muppets, made her TV debut in 1974. That same year, several *Sesame Street* characters—as huge inflated balloon floats—made their debut as part of the annual Macy's Thanksgiving Day Parade in Manhattan. (Meanwhile, Jim produced the 1970 holiday TV special

The Great Santa Claus Switch, which contained a new species of puppet characters called the Frackles.)

During these hectic years, Jim Henson and his crew were very devoted to the well-being and growth of their children's TV show. As Jim explained, "I put aside a few other areas I'd been working on, because at that point it was as if the audience wanted *Sesame Street* and it was what I should be putting my time and energy into."

However, Jim had never given up on his dream of a primetime TV show to introduce the Muppets to an adult

Education was an important part of Jim's creative efforts. Here, he and Kermit meet with children to promote the Reading is Fundamental program. (Time Life Pictures/Getty Images)

audience. This professional quest led Jim to team up with a new TV project being launched on NBC-TV by producer Lorne Michaels. It was *Saturday Night Live* (*SNL*), which debuted on October 11, 1975. The weekly show, aired live from a television studio at Manhattan's Rockefeller Center, was a sketch-comedy showcase for young comedians. The show often featured a short, offbeat film produced by Albert Brooks. The Muppets also participated in weekly sketches on *SNL*. Jim's roster of characters for the show did not include any used on *Sesame Street,* but relied on such new creations as King Ploobis, Scred, and the Mighty Favog.

After a few weeks on the air, it became evident that *Saturday Night Live* and the Muppets were not a good match. Before the end of the series' first season Henson's Muppets left *SNL*. Jim preferred devoting his and his staff's creative energies elsewhere.

Sir Lew Grade to the Rescue

Earlier in the 1970s, the Muppets had appeared as guests on a TV special starring singer/actor Julie Andrews. It was shot in England by veteran British TV producer/entrepreneur Sir Lew Grade, head of ITC Entertainment. Grade was so taken with Jim Henson's magical puppets that he suggested using them in a TV series. He was willing to do what all the American TV networks had rejected—mount an adult-oriented vehicle for the Muppets. It was agreed that 24 episodes (including two pilot segments) of the half-hour show would be produced, on condition that all the segments (1) be taped in England and (2) include a live guest star (to help TV stations who aired the syndicated show to attract needed viewership).

With new team member, David Lazer, as executive producer for this Henson Associates venture, *The Muppet Show* began filming in England. Utilizing company puppeteer regulars such as Jim Henson, Frank Oz, and Jerry Nelson and several newcomers, the roster of characters for the show was put together. They included such lovable characters as Fozzie Bear, Sgt. Floyd Pepper, Animal, Scooter, Statler, the Great Gonzo, Zoot, Mahna-Mahna, Dr. Teeth, and Beauregard. However, the favorite characters of this half-hour variety/comedy series would prove to be Kermit the Frog (as master of ceremonies) and Miss Piggy (a demanding starlet jealously in love with Kermit). Even with the economy of shooting the series in England, each episode of the elaborate and difficult series cost approximately $250,000.

The Muppet Show began airing in syndication in the United States in September 1976. Academy Award–winning performer Rita Moreno was the first guest star. In each episode, Kermit presided as the frantic emcee/manager of a bizarre troupe of shaggy animals, monsters, and even humanoid goofballs, who combined to turn their weekly musical revue into laugh-producing chaos. The show—and the series—followed Jim's firm belief that "How the character plays a particular moment on a punch line is very visual. These are not just characters up there telling jokes. The humor only holds if there's an interaction between the characters that is visual at the same time." According to Henson's vision, the new series was geared to be a "fast-paced, uninhibited, free-form farce." He also insisted upon using a laugh track for *The Muppet Show* to make the viewers feel as if they were watching a staged musical variety revue.

A New Major Hit TV Series

Although some critics gave *The Muppet Show* only fair reviews, the TV public on both sides of the Atlantic Ocean responded very favorably. Audiences soon discovered that there was always so much going on in front of the camera, that any episode could be watched several times to catch all the stage business, jokes, and subtleties. As the season proceeded, several of the warm, mischievous Muppet characters were enhanced. For example, Fozzie Bear's outlook became more positive than in earlier episodes, and Miss Piggy became more glamorous. Interactions between the puppets and the live guest stars were also smoothed out. At the Emmy Awards held on September 11, 1977,

The stars of The Muppet Show, *Jim's highly successful prime-time variety show that featured Muppets and celebrity guest stars* (Photofest)

The Muppet Show won several nominations and one prize—for Rita Moreno.

The Muppet Show went on for four additional seasons, for a total of 120 episodes. Among the live guest stars in these subsequent outings were Jim Henson's idol, Edgar Bergen (with his dummy Charlie McCarthy), Liberace, Russian ballet great Rudolf Nureyev, who executed dance steps with Miss Piggy. In the Emmy Awards covering the 1977–78 season, the show won an Emmy as Outstanding Comedy-Variety or Music Series. The program and its artists and technicians would receive many additional Emmy nominations and victories during its run, as well as winning the prestigious Peabody Award in 1979. Before the brilliant TV series ended in 1981, there would be more than 400 colorful Muppet characters populating this inventive showcase.

However, 1981 was not the end of *The Muppet Show*—which continues to this day in constant TV reruns and is available on DVD—nor was it the finale of Jim Henson's already illustrious show business career.

7

FRESH
CREATIVE
CHALLENGES

With the enormous success of *The Muppet Show* and *Sesame Street,* Jim Henson could certainly have rested on his creative and financial laurels. However, this adventurous artist had a tremendous capacity to work and inspire others and was always itching to stretch himself in new creative directions. (For example, the group prepared a HBO-cable special in 1977, *Emmet Otter's Jug-Band Christmas* which was taped in Toronto, Canada.) To remain actively involved with all his business enterprises, Henson was constantly jetting back and forth between England and the United States to hold meetings on potential new projects.

Another new venture occurred when Henson's firm—then known as HA (Henson Associates)—teamed with Sir Lew Grade and ITC to produce a feature-length film starring the world-renowned puppets. *The Muppet Movie* (1979) traced the wild adventures of Kermit, who is convinced by a talent agent to seek a Hollywood film career. On the way to California, he is joined by Miss Piggy, Fozzie, and other Muppets. Besides the contingent of beloved Muppet characters, the movie boasts a host of cameos provided by real-life performers such as Mel Brooks, Steve Martin, Richard Pryor, and Orson Welles.

Directed by James Frawley and using the principal Henson puppeteers/character voices, *The Muppet Movie* sought to advance the use of the puppets on camera. With this ambition in mind, Jim thought nothing of being encased in a watertight chamber in a swamp sequence so he could effectively operate Kermit (sitting on a log) strumming on a banjo and singing "Rainbow Connection." *Variety* called *The Muppet Movie* "a well-crafted combo of musical comedy and fantasy adventure." The trade journal also appreciated the "radio controls and other electronic gimmickry" used to showcase the Muppets in actions such as Kermit pedaling a bike and Muppets driving trucks and cars.

At this time Jim had many other projects in the works. The Muppets joined singer John Denver for a 1979 ABC-TV special *John Denver and the Muppets: A Christmas*

Together. This also led to the release of a record album of the show's songs. In addition that year, at New York's Lincoln Center an exhibit of "The Art of the Muppets" was on view.

The Dark Crystal

Another of Henson's artistic visions was to create a sophisticated feature film. In 1977, while based in England, Jim was introduced to Brian Froud, a fantasy artist who had produced a book of Celtic-inspired drawings of goblins and elves that Jim liked. Before long, Henson and Froud agreed to work on a movie project, which would become *The Dark Crystal* (1982).

It was in 1978, while waiting out a snowstorm with his daughter Cheryl at a Kennedy Airport hotel in New York, that Jim and his daughter collaborated on ideas/sketches to create the complex mystical world that would form the basis for *The Dark Crystal.* The next year, Henson purchased a former post office building in the Hampstead district of North London to be the base of operations for the film. (This headquarters, across the street from Henson's London home, would later become known as the Creature Shop.)

As pre-production got underway for *The Dark Crystal,* Jim followed his by-now traditional method of preparation. His son Brian Henson described this procedure: "He would visualize what you could do with a puppet or a person in a costume before working on it. The whole film is a series of experiments in hiding people in costumes, and creating movements that no one has ever seen before." With Jim's time divided between the ongoing *The Muppet Show,* and other activities (such as supplying the character Yoda for the 1980 film *Star Wars: Episode V—The Empire Strikes Back*), Henson hired Duncan Kenworthy to supervise the Creature Shop.

Jim was a great lover of high-tech gadgets, always rushing out to buy the latest item. It was quickly decided that the newest technological advances in filmmaking had to be applied to *The Dark Crystal.* This included the growing field of animatronics (i.e., the use of computer technology and radio controls to animate puppets or other models). As it evolved, the story for the 94-minute, PG-rated feature was a seeming blend of the world of J. R. R. Tolkien (the British author of *The Hobbit* and *The Lord of the Rings*) and the 19th-century fairytales collected by the German brothers Grimm. The movie's plot revolved around recovering a lost piece of the potent Dark Crystal in order to save the world. The cast of characters (which led to the

Creature Shop creating more than 100 different puppet characters) included such forces as the evil Skeksis, the well-meaning Mystics, and the Muppet-like Gelfings, as well as assorted monsters. Originally many of the on-camera groupings spoke in Greek or Egyptian, and subtitles were used to explain their conversations. Later, when test audiences were bothered by this distracting aspect, the foreign-language dialogue was dubbed into English.

The *New York Times* summed up the majority opinion about *The Dark Crystal,* noting that the mythical tale was "without any narrative drive whatsoever. It's without charm as well as interest." The reviewer found that most of the animated characters were "unexceptional" and that, "Most surprising is the lack of either humor or wit, especially in the designs for the mythical creatures."

Vastly disappointed by filmgoers' reception to his film, Jim realized that he should have also utilized live actors to give *The Dark Crystal* more audience interest. He also appreciated that it had been a creative mistake to devise first the elaborate setting and then the story. He decided that this process should have been done in reverse.

*Jen and Kira, two characters from Henson's 1982 feature film
The Dark Crystal (Photofest)*

Regaining His Footing

Meanwhile, the second Muppets feature film, *The Great
Muppet Caper* (1981), had been released. Directed by
Henson, the G-rated movie revolved around journalists
Kermit and Fozzie being dispatched to London to interview Lady Holiday (Diana Rigg), a fashion designer
whose costly diamond necklace has been stolen. In
England, Kermit falls in love with the designer's secre-
tary, Miss Piggy. Bolstered by performances from the
real-life actors (besides Rigg, there was Robert Morley,

John Cleese, Peter Ustinov, and Charles Grodin), the film did well with audiences. Meanwhile in the United States there were touring arena stage shows of the Muppets, retail shops that sold licensed Muppets products, the debut of *Muppet Magazine,* and more TV specials (e.g., 1981's *The Muppets Go to the Movies* and 1983's *John Denver and the Muppets: Rocky Mountain Holiday*). During this period Henson established the Henson Foundation, geared to develop and encourage public enthusiasm for the art of puppetry.

Hoping to duplicate the success of *The Muppet Show,* Henson produced a new TV series, this one for HBO. Entitled *Fraggle Rock,* the half-hour live-action puppet program debuted on January 10, 1983. It was set in the rock beneath the house of a scientist named Doc (played by Gerry Parkes). In this elaborate underground civilization dwelt three contrasting factions of creatures: the playful Fraggles, the tiny Doozers, and the oversized Gorgs. Many of the lead voices for the series were provided by Jim Henson, Jerry Nelson, Steve Whitmire, Richard Hunt, Kathryn Mullen, Dave Goelz, and Karen Prell. This appealing series, which was a plea for more harmony in our world, ran until 1987.

In September 1984, a Saturday morning cartoon series premiered entitled *Jim Henson's Muppet Babies.* The popular show, which focused on tiny tyke versions of Kermit,

Piggy, Rowlf, Gonzo, and the others, had a healthy run on CBS-TV through 1991.

Reaching Out to Please the Public

Jim was happiest when he was constantly on the run, endlessly involved in shaping new projects that utilized the newest developments in the animatronics and computer graphic imagery. Although he was approaching age 50, Henson remained tireless in his efforts. While Henson and his wife, Jane, had separated, his children (especially

Jim and characters from his successful HBO series Fraggle Rock (Photofest)

Brian) became increasingly involved in the organization's many enterprises. Keeping up the momentum, Jim and his busy staff participated in *Sesame Street Presents: Follow that Bird* (1985).

Already committed (through the Creature Shop) to provide puppets for the British-made film *Dreamchild* (1985), Jim Henson found time to propel his own next feature film, *Labyrinth,* into pre-production. The 101-minute feature was executive produced by Jim's pal, filmmaker George Lucas.

Having learned his lesson the hard way on *The Dark Crystal,* Jim was sure to include live actors in the fantasy adventure *Labyrinth.* The film tells the story of an impatient young girl who tires of babysitting her irritating baby brother. She wishes he would disappear. Her thoughtless wish is granted. Thereafter, she must solve the riddle of the labyrinth in order to rescue her sibling from the Goblin King (played by rock musician/actor David Bowie). On the way to saving her brother from being turned into a goblin, she meets a wild assortment of amazing creatures. Released by TriStar Pictures in June 1986, *Labyrinth* was not a success with critics or movie audiences, however.

While *Labyrinth* was making its way into distribution, Jim Henson turned his imagination to a new TV production, *The Storyteller.* The series was inspired by

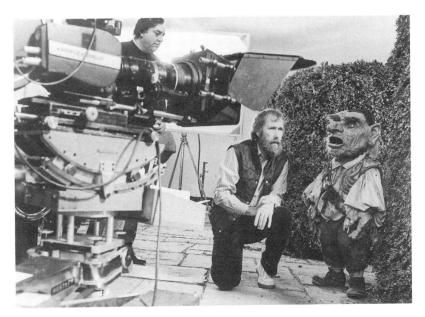

Jim on the set of his 1986 film Labyrinth (Photofest)

Henson's daughter Lisa, who had taken a course at Harvard University dealing with European folk tales. She suggested to her dad that by utilizing the talent at his Creature Shop, he could retell these lesser-known stories and incorporate the dark and brutal flavor that was so much a part of the original yarns. Hiring Anthony Minghella to write the teleplays and John Hurt to play the storyteller/narrator, the complex project got underway. While many episodes were planned, the show proved so costly and intricate that only nine episodes were shot, including the debut entry, "Hans My

Hedgehog." Jim directed one of the installments: "The Heartless Giant."

In the late 1980s these *Storyteller* shows, which featured live actors, aired over Channel 4 in the United Kingdom. It was not until April 1989 that some of these segments were shown in the United States. They were made part of NBC-TV's *The Jim Henson Hour.* This series consisted of two distinct halves: the first part resembled *The Muppet Show* and included the Muppets in skits and songs, as well as interacting with real-life celebrities. The second half of the show utilized episodes of *The Storyteller.* The short-lived series, which ended after 10 episodes in July 1989, did win Henson an Emmy Award in the category of Outstanding Directing in a Variety or Music Program.

In a Prestigious Position

In the late 1980s Jim and his staff became intrigued with the concept of educating youngsters to different styles of music. This led to the British produced 13-part TV series, *The Ghost of Faffner Hall,* and the 13-part *Jim Henson's Mother Goose Stories.* Also in 1988, the corporate name of Henson Associates officially changed its title to Jim Henson Productions.

By 1989 Jim Henson, who had been inducted into the Television Academy Hall of Fame two years earlier, could look back on an amazing array of projects in a variety of mediums. The Muppets, whether in such feature films as *The Muppets Take Manhattan* (1984), the TV-aired *A Muppet Family Christmas* (1987), or in reruns of their old small-screen series, were doing well. *Sesame Street* had been on the air continuously since 1969 and was celebrated with the 1989 NBC-TV special *Sesame Street: 20 . . . And Still Counting.*

To accommodate the constant flow of products, Henson's expansive organization had production/office facilities in England (The Creature Shop), in New York (The Muppet Shop), and in Los Angeles. The London facility, in particular, was experiencing a particular burst of creativity and profitability in the late 1980s with its contributions to such productions as *The Teenage Mutant Ninja Turtles* film/TV series and the movie *The Witches.*

By now a multimillionaire, Henson had residences in Greenwich (Connecticut), London (England), Malibu (California), Santa Fe (New Mexico), Orlando (Florida), and a three-bedroom apartment at Manhattan's Sherry-Netherland Hotel. When the workaholic Henson did take time off from his frantic business activities, he "relaxed" with whirlwind trips to Egypt (to ride camels) and to France (to hot-air balloon).

The Sudden Finale

For years, Henson's Muppets and their various offshoots were seen as strong competitors to the entertainment offerings of the Walt Disney Company. Thus, it was no surprise to the business community in 1989, when, after lengthy negotiations, a merger agreement between the two major entities got underway. While these discussions were in progress, Jim and his crew were involved in preparing *Jim Henson's Muppet*Vision 3-D* (a movie short) and two live-characters shows to be showcased at the Disney-MGM Studios Theme Park at Walt Disney World in Orlando, Florida.

On May 6, 1990, NBC-TV aired a special (*The Muppets at Walt Disney World*) hyping the teaming between these two entertainment entities. Ten days later, Jim Henson was dead at age 53.

In early May of that year Jim had developed a bothersome sore throat which he ignored. He took his daughter Cheryl to North Carolina to visit with his father and stepmother, Barbara. (Jim's mother, Betty Henson, had died many years earlier.) During this family reunion he felt extremely tired, but assumed the condition would pass. Back in New York, he had dinner with his estranged wife, Jane. (Although they were long separated, the couple remained cordial.) By early the next morning, Henson had extreme breathing problems and was rushed to New York Hospital. There physicians discovered he was suffering from a rare version of streptococcus pneumonia and convinced him to take needed medical steps. Had he sought medical treatment earlier, he might have been cured with the strong antibiotics that were administered too late.

Days later, at the Cathedral of St. John the Divine, a huge Episcopal church in uptown Manhattan near Columbia University, a crowd of nearly 5,000 mourners gathered to pay final respects to this remarkable creative artist. Because Jim had requested that his death be celebrated with a "friendly little service" (with no one wearing dreary black outfits), attendees wore colorful clothing. Many of the Muppets characters, including Big Bird, were present. The walls of the church were lined with photos of Jim. A Dixieland band played during the service. Henson's cremated ashes were scattered at his ranch outside of Santa Fe, New Mexico.

In the aftermath of Henson's death, Jim's grieving family took control of the company, with his son Brian as head of the operation. The planned merger with the Disney Company fell apart, although Jim Henson Productions and Disney's Buena Vista Home Video signed a worldwide distribution deal of home entertainment releases.

Keeping alive Jim Henson's vision, more Muppets movies were produced (1992's _Muppet Christmas Carol,_ 1996's _Muppet Treasure Island,_ and 1999's _Muppets From Space_) and new Henson-produced TV series aired (1991's _Dinosaurs,_ 1996's _Muppets Tonight,_ 1997's _Bear in the Blue Big House,_ and 1999's _Farscape_). In addition, there would be an assortment of multimedia ventures around the globe tied into the Muppets, _Sesame Street,_ and other products of Jim's creativity. Moreover, Jim's beloved The Creature Shop in England would continue to participate in a wide variety of ambitious high-tech projects for film and television.

In 2000, EM.TV & Merchandising AG, a German conglomerate, purchased the Jim Henson Company for $680 million. (None of the _Sesame Street_ properties were included in the sale.) The complex business deal soon proved thorny as the European-based EM.TV suffered a series of financial reverses. Eventually, in 2003, the Henson family bought back the Jim Henson Company from EM.TV for $84 million. In February 2004, the Walt Disney Company and the Jim Henson Company agreed to Disney purchasing from the Hensons both the Muppets and _Bear in the Big Blue House_ characters and their allied programming library. Although Brian Henson stepped down in 2002 as chairman of the Jim Henson Company, he and other family members still play key roles in the ongoing operations of the vast enterprise.

Jim Henson's Legacy

The unique and highly creative Jim Henson had a very strong impact on popular culture. Jim's work lives on, with a continuing positive effect.

Henson was the soft-spoken, whimsical soul who believed that "As children, we all live in a world of imagination of fantasy, and for some of us that world of make-believe continues into adulthood." The talented visionary once said, "Each of us expressing our own originality is the essence of art and professionalism." As for nurturing young minds with his entertaining work, Jim said, "Kids love to learn. And the learning should be exciting and fun. That's what we're out to do."

In building his tremendous show business success over the years, Jim happily teamed with many other talented craftspeople. He said once, "I like working collaboratively with people. At its best, the film and television world functions creatively this way. I have a terrific group of people who work with me, and I think of the work we do as 'our' work."

Perhaps the magical, irreverent Jim is best summed up by the observations of two of his longtime coworkers and friends. Jerry Juhl offered, "What Jim really wanted to do was to sing songs and tell stories, teach children, promote peace, save the planet, celebrate man, praise God and be silly." Frank Oz has spoken often of Henson's love

Through the legacy of his beloved creations, Jim Henson continues to educate, entertain, and inspire people around the world. (Photofest)

and respect for collaborating with other artists: "Jim was the most giving man I've ever known. He had a great generosity of spirit, of time, and of money for other people. He valued quality work, but being a good human being was just as important to him."

TIME LINE

1936 Born in Greenville, Mississippi, on September 24, the second of two sons

1948 Henson family moves permanently to Hyattsville, Maryland, so father can fulfill researching assignment for the U.S. Department of Agriculture

1954 Graduates from Northwestern High School and enters University of Maryland at College Park; makes first TV appearance on *The Junior Good Morning Show* at WTOP in Washington, D.C.

1955 The humorous puppet show *Sam and Friends* airs twice daily on WRC-TV, Washington, D.C.; college friend Jane Nebel assists Henson with show

1956 Older brother Paul Jr. killed in a car accident; guest appearances on TV's *Tonight* and *The Arthur Godfrey Show*

1957 Tapes first TV commercial (for Wilkins Coffee)

1958   Makes European tour to learn more about puppetry; *Hansel and Gretel* production abandoned;
Sam and Friends earns local Emmy Award; incorpo-
rates company as Muppets Inc.

1959   Marries Jane Nebel on May 28

1960   First of the Muppets' many appearances on NBC-
TV's *Today* show; daughter Lisa born

1961   *Sam and Friends* ends TV run; daughter Cheryl born

1962   TV pilot *Tales of the Tinkerdee* taped in Atlanta,
Georgia; Rowlf the Dog puppet appears in Purina
dog food TV commercial

1963   Muppets operation moves to Manhattan; Rowlf the
Dog (with Henson as puppeteer) becomes series
regular on *The Jimmy Dean Show* (ABC-TV); son
Brian born

1964   Begin production of experimental short film *Time
Piece* (1965), which will be Oscar-nominated

1965   Develops business meetings films for corporations;
Hey, Cinderella! TV pilot taped; son John born

1966   First of Muppets' many appearances on CBS-TV's
The Ed Sullivan Show; makes business films for
IBM

1967   Works on *Cyclia,* a multimedia nightclub project later abandoned; Rowlf the Dog is host of CBS-TV's *Our Place* series

1968   Tapes NET-TV special, *Muppets on Puppets*; short film *Youth '68* airs on *NBC Experiment in Television*; TV special *Hey, Cinderella!* shot in Toronto, Canada

1969   Joins with Children's Television Workshop to make pilot and initial episode of PBS-TV's series *Sesame Street* which debuts on November 10; short film *The Cube* airs on *NBC Experiment in Television*

1970   *The Great Santa Claus Switch* TV special taped; *Sesame Street* releases first record album; daughter Heather born

1971   Muppets makes guest appearances on assorted TV series (e.g., *The Flip Wilson Show*) and specials (e.g., *Pure Goldie* [Hawn]); Muppets part of Nancy Sinatra's Las Vegas casino club act

1972   TV specials: *The Frog Prince* (syndicated) and *Muppet Musicians of Bremen* (syndicated)

1973   TV special: *The Muppets Valentine Special* (ABC-TV)

1975   Muppet characters are regulars on premiere season of *Saturday Night Live* (NBC-TV)

1976 Syndicated *The Muppet Show* begins taping in England with U.S. premiere on September 26

1977 TV special: *Emmet Otter's Jug-Band Christmas* taped in Toronto, Canada; new Henson offices acquired in Manhattan

1978 Pre-production work begins in England for *The Dark Crystal* feature film; *The Muppet Show* wins first of several Emmy Awards

1979 Purchases old building in North London which becomes The Creature Shop; feature film: *The Muppet Movie* (Associated Film Distribution); TV specials: *John Denver and The Muppets: A Christmas Together* (ABC-TV) and *The Muppets Go Hollywood* (CBS-TV)

1981 *The Muppet Show* ends five-year run; feature film: *The Great Muppet Caper* (Universal/Associated Film Distribution); TV specials: *Here Come the Puppets* (syndicated) and *The Muppets Go to the Movies* (ABC-TV)

1982 Henson Foundation established to promote art of puppetry; feature film: *The Dark Crystal* (Universal/Associated Film Distribution); TV special: *The Fantastic Miss Piggy Show* (ABC-TV)

1983   TV series: *Fraggle Rock* (HBO); TV specials: *Big Bird in China* (NBC) and *John Denver and the Muppets: Rocky Mountain Holiday* (ABC)

1984   Feature film: *The Muppets Take Manhattan* (TriStar); TV series: *Jim Henson's Muppet Babies* (CBS); TV special: *The Bells of Fraggle Rock* (HBO)

1985   *The Muppets: A Celebration of 30 Years* taped in Toronto, Canada

1986   Feature film: *Labyrinth* (TriStar); TV special: *The Tale of the Bunny Picnic* (1986)

1987   Inducted into Television Academy Hall of Fame; *Puppetman* TV pilot taped in Canada; TV series: (animated) *Fraggle Rock* (NBC) and *Jim Henson's The Storyteller* (NBC); TV special: *A Muppet Family Christmas* (ABC)

1988   Henson Associates becomes Jim Henson Productions

1989   Henson Productions begin merger negotiations with the Walt Disney Company; TV series: *The Ghost of Faffner Hall* (HBO); TV special: *Sesame Street: 20 . . . and Still Counting* (NBC)

1990   Production begins on *Jim Henson's Muppet*Vision 3-D* film short for Walt Disney World in Florida; dies

May 16; merger with the Walt Disney Company abandoned; TV series: *Jim Henson's Mother Goose Stories* (Disney); TV specials: *The Muppets at Walt Disney World* (NBC) and *The Muppets Celebrate Jim Henson* (CBS)

1991   Son Brian named president of Jim Henson Productions; legacy of Jim Henson continues with feature films and TV series

HOW TO BECOME A FILMMAKER

THE JOB

Filmmakers, also called film directors, bear ultimate responsibility for the tone and quality of the films they work on. They interpret the stories and narratives presented in scripts and coordinate the filming of their interpretations. They are involved in preproduction, production, and postproduction. They audition, select, and rehearse the acting crew; they work on matters regarding set designs, musical scores, and costumes; and they decide on details such as where scenes should be shot, what backgrounds might be needed, and how special effects could be employed.

The director of a film often works with a casting director, who is in charge of auditioning performers. The casting director pays close attention to attributes of the performers such as physical appearance, quality of voice, and acting ability and experience, and then presents to the director a list of suitable candidates for each role.

One of the most important aspects of the film director's job is working with the performers. Directors have their own styles of extracting accurate emotion and performances from cast members, but they must be dedicated to this goal.

Two common techniques that categorize directors' styles are montage and mise-en-scene. Montage directors are concerned primarily with using editing techniques to produce desired results; they consider it important to focus on how individual shots will work when pieced together with others. Consider Alfred Hitchcock, who directed the production of one scene in Psycho, for example, by filming discrete shots in a bathroom and then editing in dialogue, sound effects, and music to create tremendous suspense. Mise-en-scene directors are more concerned with the pre-editing phase, focusing on the elements of angles, movement, and design one shot at a time, as Orson Welles did. Many directors combine elements of both techniques in their work.

The film's art director creates set design concepts and chooses shoot locations. He or she meets with the filmmaker and producer to set budgets and schedules and then accordingly coordinates the construction of sets. Research is done on the period in which the film is to take place, and experts are consulted to help create appropriate architectural and environmental styles. The art director also is often involved in design ideas for costumes, makeup and hairstyles, photographic effects, and other elements of the film's production.

The director of photography, or cinematographer, is responsible for organizing and implementing the actual camera work. Together with the filmmaker, he or she interprets scenes and decides on appropriate camera motion to achieve desired results. The director of photography determines the amounts of natural and artificial lighting required for each shoot and such technical factors as the type of film to be used, camera angles and distance, depth of field, and focus.

Motion pictures are usually filmed out of sequence, meaning that the ending might be shot first and scenes from the middle of the story might not be filmed until the end of production. Directors are responsible for scheduling each day's sequence of scenes; they coordinate filming so that scenes using the same set and performers will be filmed together. In addition to conferring with the art director and the director of photography, filmmakers meet with technicians and crew members to advise on and approve final scenery, lighting, props, and other necessary equipment. They are also involved with final approval of costumes, choreography, and music.

After all the scenes have been shot, postproduction begins. The director works with picture and sound editors to cut apart and piece together the final reels. The film editor shares the director's vision about the picture and assembles shots according to that overall idea, synchronizing film with voice and sound tracks produced by the sound editor and music editor.

While the director supervises all major aspects of film production, various assistants help throughout the process. In a less creative position than the filmmaker's, the first assistant director organizes various practical matters involved during the shooting of each scene. The second assistant director is a coordinator who works as a liaison among the production office, the first assistant director, and the performers. The second unit director coordinates sequences such as scenic inserts and action shots that do not involve the main acting crew.

REQUIREMENTS

High School

Film directors' careers are rather nontraditional. There is no standard training outline involved, and no normal progression up a movie industry ladder leading to the director's job. At the very least, a high school diploma, while not technically required if you wish to become a director, will still probably be indispensable to you in terms of the background and education it signifies. As is true of all artists, especially those in a medium as widely disseminated as film, you will need to have rich and varied experience in order to create works that are intelligently crafted and speak to people of many different backgrounds. In high school, courses in English, art, theater, and history will give you a good foundation. Further, a high school diploma will be necessary if you decide to go on to film school. Be active in school and community drama productions, whether as performer, set designer, or cue-card holder.

Postsecondary Training

In college and afterward, take film classes and volunteer to work on other students' films. Dedication, talent, and experience have always been indispensable to a director. No doubt it is beneficial to become aware of one's passion for film as early as possible. Woody Allen, for example, recognized early in his life the importance that motion pictures held for him, but he worked as a magician, jazz clarinet player, joke writer, and stand-up comic before ever directing films. Allen has taken few film courses in his life.

On the other hand, many successful directors such as Francis Ford Coppola and Martha Coolidge have taken the formal film school route. There are more than 500 film studies programs offered by schools of higher education throughout the United States, including those considered to be the five most reputable: those of the American Film Institute in Los Angeles (AFI), Columbia University in New York City, New York University (NYU), the University of California at Los Angeles (UCLA), and the University of Southern California (USC). These schools have film professionals on their faculties and provide a very visible stage for student talent, being located in the two film-business hot spots, California and New York. (The tuition for film programs offered elsewhere, however, tends to be much less expensive than at these schools.)

Film school offers overall formal training, providing an education in fundamental directing skills by working with student productions. Such education is rigorous, but in addition to teaching skills it provides aspiring directors with peer groups and a network of contacts with students, faculty, and guest speakers that can be of help after graduation.

The debate continues regarding what is more influential in a directing career: film school or personal experience. Some say that it is possible for creative people to land directing jobs without having gone through a formal program. Competition is so pervasive in the industry that even film school graduates find jobs scarce (only 5 to 10 percent of the 26,000 students who graduate from film schools each year find jobs in the industry). Martha Coolidge, for instance, made independent films for 10 years before directing a Hollywood movie.

Other Requirements

Konstantin Stanislavsky had a passion for his directorial work in the theater, believing that it was an art of immense social importance. Today's motion picture directors must have similar inspiration and possibly even greater creative strength, because of the many responsibilities involved in directing modern films.

EXPLORING

If you are a would-be director, the most obvious opportunity for exploration lies in your own imagination. Being drawn to films and captivated by the process of how they are made is the beginning of the filmmaker's journey.

In high school and beyond, carefully study and pay attention to motion pictures. Watch them at every opportunity, both at the theater and at home. Study your favorite television shows to see what makes them interesting. Two major trade publications to read are *Variety* (http://www.variety.com) and *Hollywood Reporter* (http://www.hollywoodreporter. com). The Directors Guild of America's official publication *DGA Magazine* contains much information on the industry. If you are unable to find this magazine at a public library or bookstore, visit the DGA website to read sample articles (http://www.dga.org). Also, the book *How to Make It in Hollywood: All the Right Moves* (Linda Buzzell, 1996, Harper Perennial) is a very good informal guide that presents insider tips on such factors as "schmoozing" and chutzpah (self-confidence) as well as an extensive list of valuable resources.

During summers, many camps and workshops offer programs for high school students interested in film work. For example, UCLA presents its Media Workshops for students aged 14 to 24. Classes there focus on mass media production, including film, TV, and video. For information, contact the Media Workshops Foundation, Tel: 800-223-4561, http://www.mediaworkshops.org/foundation.

EMPLOYERS

Employment as a film or television director is usually on a freelance or contractual basis. Directors find work, for example, with film studios (both major and independent), at television stations and cable networks, through advertising agencies, with record companies, and through the creation of their own independent film projects.

STARTING OUT

It is considered difficult to begin as a motion picture director. With nontraditional steps to professional status, the occupation poses challenges for those seeking employment. However, there is somewhat solid advice for those who wish to direct motion pictures.

Many current directors began their careers in other film industry professions, such as acting or writing. Consider

Jodie Foster, who appeared in 30 films and dozens of television productions before she went on to direct her first motion picture at the age of 28. Obviously it helps to grow up near the heart of "Tinseltown" and to have the influence of one's family spurring one on. The support of family and friends is often cited as an essential element in shaping the confidence you need to succeed in the industry.

As mentioned earlier, film school is an ideal place for making contacts in the industry. Often, contacts are the essential factor in getting a job; many Hollywood insiders agree that it's not what you know but whom you know that will get you in. Networking often leads to good opportunities at various types of jobs in the industry. Many professionals recommend that those who want to become directors should go to Los Angeles or New York, find any industry-related job, continue to take classes, and keep their eyes and ears open for news of job openings, especially with those professionals who are admired for their talent.

Be aware of the Assistant Directors Training Program of the Directors Guild of America. This program provides an excellent opportunity to those without industry connections to work on film and television productions. The program is based at two locations, New York City for the East Coast program and Sherman Oaks, California, for the West Coast program. Trainees receive hands-on experience, through placement with major studios or on television movies and series, and education, through mandatory seminars. The East Coast program requires trainees to complete up to 350 days of on-set production work; the West Coast program requires 400 days. While they are working, trainees are paid, beginning with a weekly salary of $487 in the East and $521 in the West. Once trainees have completed their program, they become freelance second assistant directors and can join the guild. The competition is extremely stiff for these positions; each location usually accepts 20 or fewer trainees from among some 800 to 1,200 applicants each year.

Keep in mind that major studios in Hollywood are not the only place where directors work. Directors also work on documentaries, on television productions, and with various types of video presentations, from music to commercials. Honing skills at these types of jobs is beneficial for those still intent on directing the big screen.

ADVANCEMENT

In the motion picture industry, advancement often comes with recognition. Directors who work on well-received movies are given awards as well as further job offers. Probably the most glamorized trophy is the Academy Award: the Oscar. Oscars are awarded in 24 categories, including one for best achievement in directing, and are given annually at a gala to recognize the outstanding accomplishments of those in the field.

Candidates for Oscars are usually judged by their peers. Directors who have not worked on films popular enough to have made it in Hollywood should nevertheless seek recognition from reputable organizations. One such group is the National Endowment for the Arts, an independent agency of the U.S. government that supports and awards artists, including those who work in film. The endowment provides financial assistance in the form of fellowships and grants to those seen as contributing to the excellence of arts in the country.

EARNINGS

Directors' salaries vary greatly. Most Hollywood film directors are members of the Directors Guild of America, and salaries (as well as hours of work and other employment conditions) are usually negotiated by this union. Generally, contracts provide for minimum weekly salaries and follow a basic trend depending on the cost of the picture being produced: for film budgets over $1.5 million, the weekly salary is about $8,000; for budgets of $500,000 to $1.5 million, it is $5,800 per week; and for budgets under $500,000, the weekly salary is $5,100. Motion picture art directors earn an average weekly salary of about $1,850; directors of photography, $2,000. Keep in mind that because directors and many other workers in the film industry are freelancers, they may have no income for many weeks out of the year.

Although contracts usually provide only for the minimum rate of pay, most directors earn more, and they often negotiate extra conditions. Woody Allen, for example, takes the minimum salary required by the union for directing a film but also receives at least 10 percent of the film's gross receipts.

Salaries for directors who work in television vary greatly based on type of project and employer and on whether the director is employed as a freelancer or as a salaried employee. A director at a small-market station may average as little as $28,000 per year, while a director employed by a larger network affiliate may make up to $120,000 annually. The U.S. Department of Labor reports that the median annual salary of film, stage and radio directors and producers was $52,840 in 2004.

WORK ENVIRONMENT

The work of the director is considered glamorous and prestigious, and of course directors have been known to become quite famous. But directors work under great stress, meeting deadlines, staying within budgets, and resolving problems among staff. "Nine-to-five" definitely does not describe a day in the life of a director; 16-hour days (and more) are not uncommon. Because directors are ultimately responsible for so much, schedules often dictate that they be immersed in their work around the clock, from preproduction to final cut. Nonetheless, those able to make it in the industry find their work to be extremely enjoyable and satisfying.

OUTLOOK

According to the U.S. Department of Labor, employment for motion picture and television directors is expected to grow about as fast as the average for all occupations through 2012. This forecast is based on the increasing global demand for films and television programming made in the United States as well as continuing U.S. demand for home video and DVD rentals. However, competition is extreme and turnover is high. Most positions in the motion picture industry are held on a freelance basis. As is the case with most film industry workers, directors are usually hired to work on one film at a time. After a film is completed, new contacts must be made for further assignments.

Television offers directors a wider variety of employment opportunities such as directing sitcoms, made-for-television movies, newscasts, commercials, even music videos. Cable television networks are proliferating, and directors are needed to help create original programming for them. Half of all television directors work as freelancers. This number is predicted to rise as more cable networks and production companies attempt to cut costs by hiring directors on a project-to-project basis.

TO LEARN MORE ABOUT FILMMAKERS

BOOKS

Currell, David. *Puppets and Puppet Theater*. Wiltshire, U.K.: Crowood Press, 1999.

Dannenbaum, Jed, Carroll Hodge, and Doe Mayer. *Creative Filmmaking from the Inside Out: Five Keys to the Art of Making Inspired Movies and Television*. New York: Fireside, 2003.

Katz, Steven. *Film Directing: Shot by Shot*. Studio City, Calif.: Michael Wiese Productions, 1991.

Lanier, Troy, and Clay Nichols. *Filmmaking for Teens*. Studio City, Calif.: Michael Wiese Productions, 2005.

Shaner, Peter, and Gerald Everett Jones. *Digital Filmmaking for Teens*. Boston: Course Technology PTR, 2004.

ORGANIZATIONS AND WEBSITES

For information on the AFI Conservatory, AFI workshops, AFI awards, and other film and television news, visit the AFI website or contact

American Film Institute (AFI)
2021 North Western Avenue
Los Angeles, CA 90027
Tel: 323-856-7600
http://www.afi.com

For information on scholarships and grants, interest divisions, and publications, contact

Broadcast Education Association
1771 N Street, NW
Washington, DC 20036-2891
Tel: 888-380-7222
Email: beainfo@beaweb.org
http://www.beaweb.org

Visit the DGA website to read selections from the *DGA Magazine,* get industry news, and find links to film schools and film festivals.

Directors Guild of America (DGA)
7920 Sunset Boulevard
Los Angeles, CA 90046
Tel: 310-289-2000
http://www.dga.org

For more information about DGA's Assistant Directors Training Program, visit these websites.

East Coast Program

http://www.dgatrainingprogram.org

West Coast Program

http://www.trainingplan.org

HOW TO BECOME A TELEVISION DIRECTOR

THE JOB

The television director's responsibilities are varied and often depend on the project. For example, the director of a TV movie, documentary, or an episode of a series will have more control over the final production than the director of a news broadcast or a live event. The TV director working on a movie will use a script, go through rehearsals with actors, and shoot and reshoot scenes from many perspectives. To achieve the intended mood of the piece—such as dark and gloomy for a mystery—the director carefully orchestrates the work of lighting and sound technicians, camera operators, and editors. With such a production, the director can take the time to polish the final product that the audience will see.

A director covering a live event, such as a football game, has much less control over the outcome. In this case, the director only gets one chance at broadcasting the game. The director's responsibilities may include working with announcers to make sure their equipment is functioning properly; stationing camera operators so that they are positioned correctly to cover any possible play the teams might make; and being ready to introduce graphics, such as charts with player statistics. The director has little room for error when covering a live event.

Richard Perry, a director/editor for WWAY TV-3 in Wilmington, North Carolina, directs the 5:30 P.M. newscast. News directors may need to combine working from a script and an arranged order of stories with the unpredictability of covering a live event. In addition, the news director's job isn't limited to the actual broadcast; he or she must also direct promotional segments, news updates, and some videotaped segments to accompany the live reports during broadcast. Although Perry directs the evening news, he reports to work at 5 A.M. to help prepare for the daily morning show as well as to direct the various updates and promotions to be broadcast throughout the day.

One of the first things Perry does every morning is to make the graphics for the morning news and, as he says,

"I prep the 'supers'." Supers are superimposed words that run across the TV screen and provide information such as the names of interview subjects. The newsroom sends a printed list of these supers to Perry. He then types the names and titles into the chryon (the character generator), making sure everything is spelled correctly and in the right order. From 6 to 7 A.M., Perry runs the chryon for the morning show. This involves hitting the control for running the words across the screen at the right time. From 7 to 8:30 A.M., Perry directs the local weather and news cut-ins for broadcasting during *Good Morning America.*

After his morning work, Perry is usually able to take a break. He returns to the station mid-afternoon and often spends a couple of hours working on commercial production, then he begins preproduction for the evening news. "We make graphics for over-the-shoulder shots," he explains, "and put boards on tape for the news editors to put in their stories." Boards are graphics and lists of information. These boards are videotaped, then edited by the reporter directly into news packages (or self-contained stories on tape, consisting of the reporter's audio and edited video). In the half hour before the evening news, Perry goes over the script, which has information about the order in which stories will be shown and who is covering them.

During the broadcast, the director typically sits in the control room and wears a headset through which he or she communicates with the producer and TV crew. The director gives orders to keep the broadcast running smoothly and on time. Large TV stations have both a director and a technical director—a member of the technical crew who works directly with the cameras and other equipment and may make adjustments on the control board. But in a smaller station, like Perry's, directors take on many responsibilities. "I sit in front of the switcher," Perry says, "and tell everyone what to do and push all the right buttons at the right time so the show looks smooth." He tells the camera people what to shoot next and calls for tapes to be played (or "rolled") during the broadcast.

Freelance directors may work on live or taped productions. In addition to their responsibilities as directors—coordinating the work of crews, deciding on shots, overseeing editing—they may also need to take on many other elements involved in production. For example, they may need to work on getting funding for a project, hiring writers and assistants, or setting up locations for filming. They may even be involved in publicizing the project and entering it in festivals or competitions. In addition to all these responsibilities, freelance directors must also continually promote themselves and look for new projects to work on. The workflow for a freelance director can be unpredictable. They often take on a variety of projects, covering anything from sporting events to beauty pageants, in order to maintain a steady work schedule.

REQUIREMENTS

High School

The sooner you can get to know a camera and how to set up interesting shots, the better. If your high school offers courses about media or television production, be sure to take those. You should also consider taking photography classes that will teach you about the composition of an image. Take English and journalism classes that will hone your communication skills and give you practice completing assignments on a deadline. Computer classes that teach you how to work with graphics programs will be beneficial. If you are considering working as a freelancer, take mathematics, business, or accounting classes to help you manage your business. If you're interested in live directing and working with actors and story scripts, take drama classes to gain experience in this area.

Postsecondary Training

Although a college degree isn't necessarily required of a TV director, it does give you an edge in the workplace. Also, many colleges have internship programs and career services that can help you get your foot in the door of the professional world. If you're interested in working for a TV news station, you should apply to the broadcast departments of journalism schools.

If you're interested in directing dramas or sitcoms for network and cable TV, you may want to enroll in a drama school to develop a theater background and experience working with scripts and actors. A number of universities and colleges also offer film studies programs or courses on television broadcast production. Your guidance counselor should be able to help you locate these. Also, do research on your own by checking out school websites and reading books such as *The Complete Guide to American Film Schools and Cinema and Television Courses* by Ernest Pintoff (New York: Penguin, 1994).

No matter what college program you enroll in, however, one of your top goals should be to gain practical hands-on experience through an internship at a TV station. You will probably not be paid for your work, but you may be able to get course credit. Some schools offer internship opportunities.

Organizations may also be a source of information on internships. The Radio-Television News Directors Association, for example, offers a limited number of scholarships and internships. The Directors Guild of America sponsors several training programs. One of these, the New York Assistant Director Training Program, lasts two years and gives the participants experience shooting on locations primarily in the New York City area. Competition for these programs is extremely fierce. A summer fellowship at the International Radio and Television Society offers an all-expense paid program, which includes career-planning advice and practical experience at a New York-based corporation. They also offer a minority career workshop, which brings college students to New York for orientation in electronic media.

Other Requirements

Those who want to be television directors should be strong leaders. "You have to be in order to pull together so many people to this one common goal: getting the show on the air cleanly," says Richard Perry. Directors also must be able to concentrate in a hectic environment. Perry notes, "I have an ability to focus on whatever is before me and to block out everything else that is unnecessary."

A director also needs self-confidence as well as the ability to work with other people. Personality conflicts sometimes arise between producers and directors or other members of the production team. The director needs to be able to mediate differences and bring people together. As a director, you might need to join a union. Directors working at network stations and for major markets typically have union membership.

EXPLORING

Join your high school newspaper staff to become familiar with reporting and editing. Volunteer to act as a staff photographer. If your high school has its own TV station, join the production crew. You might be able to videotape school events or work on the school newscast. Also, consider getting involved with the drama club. You may not want to be the star of the school play, but you can be involved in production work and may be able to videotape the play for the drama archives.

Contact a local TV station and ask for a tour of the facilities. Explain that you are interested in working as a director and ask to meet with one during your tour. Or, set up a separate appointment for an informational interview with a director. Go to the interview prepared to ask questions about the work and the director's experience. People are often happy to talk about their work if you show a genuine interest.

EMPLOYERS

Television directors may work as salaried full-time employees for network or network-affiliated stations, cable stations, businesses, or agencies, or they may work as freelancers. Freelancers are not full-time employees of a particular company. Instead, freelancers work on a project-by-project basis for different employers, for example doing one project for a network and another for an advertising agency.

STARTING OUT

The position of director is not an entry-level job. You will need to work your way up through the ranks, gaining experience and knowledge along the way. Internships provide the best way to enter this competitive field. The internship gives you hands-on experience and the opportunity to make contacts within the industry. Richard Perry's internship as a production assistant during college led to his permanent position with WWAY-TV. "I gradually worked my way up through prompter, camera, tapes, audio, and finally I was a director." Perry also worked part time for the station for three-and-a-half years before being hired full time.

Other starting-out possibilities include working as an assistant for a freelance director or video production company. Be prepared to take any position that will give you hands-on experience with cameras and production, even if it's only on a part-time or temporary basis.

ADVANCEMENT

Advancement for television directors depends somewhat on their individual goals. One director might consider it an advancement to move from general TV programming to special interest programming. Another might feel that becoming a full-time freelancer is an advancement. Those who work at small stations tend to advance by relocating and working for larger stations. "If I want to move up as a director," Richard Perry says, "I'll have to move up to a larger market, maybe Charlotte or Raleigh." Such a move would mean receiving a larger salary and require overseeing a bigger staff.

EARNINGS

Salaries vary greatly for TV directors and are determined by a number of factors. A director of a newscast at a small TV station will probably be at the low end of the scale, while a director working on a hit series for a network may earn hundreds of thousands of dollars a year. A freelance director working project-to-project may earn a great deal one year and much less the following year.

According to the Bureau of Labor Statistics, the median yearly income for all producers and directors was $52,840 in 2004. The lowest 10 percent earned less than $24,750; the highest 10 percent earned more than $130,330. A 2001 salary survey by the Radio-Television News Directors Association found that television news directors had salaries that ranged from $18,000 to $250,000. Their median annual salary was $64,000. Assistant news directors earned between $19,000 to $150,000. The median salary was $57,000.

Directors who work full-time for stations or other organizations generally receive benefits such as health insurance and paid vacation and sick days.

WORK ENVIRONMENT

A TV station is a busy and exciting place where no two days are exactly alike. If the director is working on a live event, the atmosphere may be stressful and somewhat chaotic as he or she makes snap decisions, calls up the correct graphics, and keeps the show within the time limits. A director working on a taped project that will air at a later date may feel somewhat less "on air" stress; however, this director must also constantly pay attention to numerous production details, staying on budget and resolving problems among the staff. Because the director is responsible for clarifying what everyone's responsibilities for a project are, he or she may need to mediate in a tense situation. "Nine-to-five" definitely does not describe a day in the life of a director; 12-hour days (and more) are not uncommon. Because directors are ultimately responsible for so much, schedules often dictate that they become immersed in their work around the clock, from preproduction to final cut. Nonetheless, those able to make it in the industry find their work to be extremely enjoyable and satisfying.

OUTLOOK

The U.S. Department of Labor predicts that employment growth for actors, producers, and directors will increase at an average rate through 2012. Those wanting to become directors should realize that many see the television industry as a glamorous field, and there will always be stiff competition for jobs.

More TV programs are produced now than ever before, and this number should continue to grow. New technology will allow cable stations to offer hundreds of additional channels and therefore need more original programming. Also, as more businesses and organizations recognize that TV and video productions can educate the public about their work as well as train employees, they will need directors' services to complete new projects.

Newsrooms provide TV stations with healthy profits every year, and this is not expected to change. Therefore, directors will continue to be in demand to direct newscasts. Directors of traditionally less-recognized forms, such as commercials and music videos, are beginning to receive more name recognition.

In the future, the number of TV directors who work freelance will likely increase. As productions become more costly and as smaller networks produce original programming, hiring directors on a project-to-project basis is becoming more economical.

TO LEARN MORE ABOUT TELEVISION DIRECTORS

BOOKS

Cury, Ivan. *Directing & Producing for Television: A Format Approach.* 2d ed. Burlington, Mass.: Focal Press, 2001.

Trottier, David. *The Screenwriter's Bible.* 4th ed. Los Angeles: Silman-James Press, 2005.

Underdahl, Ken. *Digital Video For Dummies.* 3d ed. Hoboken, N.J.: For Dummies, 2003.

Weston, Judith. *Directing Actors: Creating Memorable Performances for Film and Television.* Studio City, Calif.: Michael Wiese Productions, 1999.

Zettl, Herbert. *Television Production Handbook.* 9th ed. Belmont, Calif.: Wadsworth, 2005.

ORGANIZATIONS AND WEBSITES

To learn more about the industry and DGA-sponsored training programs and to read selected articles from *DGA Magazine,* contact

Directors Guild of America (DGA)

7920 Sunset Boulevard

Los Angeles, CA 90046

Tel: 310-289-2000

http://www.dga.org

For more information on fellowships, contact

International Radio and Television Society

420 Lexington Avenue, Suite 1601

New York, NY 10170

Tel: 212-867-6650

http://www.irts.org

This organization for electronic media news professionals has information on internships, scholarships, and the news industry. The website has a "bookstore" featuring titles of interest to students and professionals involved in the industry.

Radio-Television News Directors Association

1600 K Street, NW, Suite 700

Washington, DC 20006-2838

Tel: 202-659-6510

Email: rtnda@rtnda.org

http://www.rtnda.org

This website contains links to numerous television-related sites and lists colleges and universities worldwide that offer training in television broadcast production.

CineMedia

http://www.cinemedia.org

TO LEARN MORE ABOUT JIM HENSON

BOOKS

Aaseng, Nathan. *Jim Henson: Muppet Master*. Minneapolis, Minn.: Lerner, 1988.*

Bacon, Matt. *No Strings Attached: The Inside Story of Jim Henson's Creature Shop*. New York: Macmillan, 1997.

Canizares, Susan, and Samantha Berger. *Meet Jim Henson*. New York: Scholastic, 1999.*

Durrett, Deanne, *Jim Henson*. San Diego, Calif.: Lucent, 1994.*

Editors. *1997 Current Biography Yearbook*. Bronx, N.Y.: H. W. Wilson, 1997.

Erickson, Hal. *Syndicated Television The First Forty Years, 1947–1987*. Jefferson, N.C.: McFarland, 1989.

Finch, Christopher. *Jim Henson: The Works—The Art, the Magic, the Imagination.* New York: Random House, 1983.

Gikow, Louise. *Meet Jim Henson.* New York: Random House, 1993.*

Goldberg, Lee. *Unsold Television Pilots: 1955 Through 1988.* Jefferson, N.C.: McFarland, 1990.

Gourse, Leslie. *Jim Henson: Young Puppeteer.* Aladdin/ Simon & Schuster, 2000.*

Grant, John. *Masters of Animation.* Collingdale, Pa.: Diane, 2001.

Inches, Alison. *Jim Henson's Design and Doodles: A Muppet Sketchbook.* New York: Harry N. Abrams, 2001.

Italia, Bob. *The Muppets.* Edina, Minn.: Abdo & Daughters, 1991.*

McMurray, Emily, ed. *Contemporary Theatre, Film and Television, Vol. 11.* Farmington Hills, Mich.: Gale, 1993.

Petrucelli, Rita, and Luciano Lazzarino. *Jim Henson: Creator of the Muppets.* Vero Beach, Fla.: Rourke, 1989.*

St. Pierre, Stephanie. *The Story of Jim Henson, Creator of the Muppets.* New York: Yearling/Dell, 1991.*

Terrace, Vincent. *Television Specials: 1939–1993.* Jefferson, N.C.: McFarland, 1995.

Woods, Geraldine. *Jim Henson: From Puppets to Muppets.* Minneapolis, Minn.: Dillon, 1987.*

*Young adult books

WEBSITES

The Complete Henson Database
http://www.hensondb.tk

E! Online
http://www.eonline.com

Internet Movie Database
http://www.imdb.com

The Jim Henson Foundation
http://www.hensonfoundation.org

Muppet Central
http://www.muppetcentral.com

Muppets.com
http://muppets.go.com/main.html

Puppeteers of America
http://www.puppeteers.org

Sesame Street
http://pbskids.org/sesame

Sesame Workshop (formerly Children's Television Workshop)
http://www.sesameworkshop.org/aboutus/inside_ataglance.php

The Unofficial Web Guide to Muppet People, Productions and Characters

http://www.punchandjewelry.com/legacy/html/mpindex.htm

INDEX

Page numbers in *italics* indicate illustrations.

A

Afternoon (television show) 29
Allen, Steve 30, 38
Animal (puppet) 68
Animatronics 75
Arthur Godfrey's Talent Scouts (television program) 17
"The Art of the Muppets" (art show) 74

B

Baird, Bill and Cora 19, 25
Baskerville (puppet) 52
Baum, L. Frank 11
Bear in the Big Blue House (television program) 86
Beauregard (puppet) 68
Bergen, Edgar 13, *14*, 25, 70
Berle, Milton ("Uncle Miltie") 18

Bert and Ernie (puppets) 63, *64*
Big Bird (puppet) 1, 40, 63, *64*, 65, 85
Brillstein, Bernie 50
Brooks, Albert 67
Brown, Sarah ("Dear") (grandmother) 8–10

C

Charlie McCarthy (puppet) 13, *14*, 25, 70
Children's Television Workshop (CTW) 60–61
Christian Science Monitor (newspaper) 9
Cleese, John 78
Connell, Dave 60
Cookie Monster (puppet) 1, 63, *64*
Cooney, Joan Ganz 59–60
The Creature Shop 74–76, 80–81, 83, 86
The Cube (film) 56
Cyclia (projected film) 56

D

The Dark Crystal (film)
74–77, 80
Dean, Jimmy 52–53
Denver, John 73–74, 78
Dinosaurs (television program) 86
Dr. Teeth (puppet) 68
Doozers (puppets) 78
Dreamchild (film) 80

E

Edgar Bergen and Charlie McCarthy Show (radio program) 13
The Ed Sullivan Show (television program) 56–57
Elmo (puppet) 1
Emmet Otter's Jug-Band Christmas (television program) 72
EM.TV & Merchandising AG (company) 86
Ernie (puppet) 1
Experiments in Television (television series) 56

F

Farscape (television series) 86
Fozzie Bear (puppet) 1, 68–69, *70*, 73, 77
Fraggle Rock (television program) 78, *79*

Fraggles (puppets) 78, *79*
Frawley, James 73
The Frog Prince (television program) 58
Froud, Brian 74

G

Gelfings (puppets) 76
The Ghost of Faffner Hall (television series) 82
Gibbon, Sam 60
The Goblin King (live character) 80
Goelz, Dave 78
Gorgs (puppets) 78
Grade, Sir Lew 67–68, 73
The Great Gonzo (puppet) 1, 68, 79
The Great Muppet Caper (film) 77
The Great Santa Claus Switch (television program) 66
The Green Hornet (radio program) 12
Grimm, Brothers (Jacob and Wilhelm) 75
Grodin, Charles 78

H

Hank (puppet) 35
Hansel and Gretel (projected puppet program) 44
"Hans My Hedgehog" (television episode) 82–83

"The Heartless Giant" (television episode) 83

Henson, Barbara (stepmother) 84

Henson, Brian (son) 53, 75, 80, 85–87

Henson, Cheryl (daughter) 47, 74, 84

Henson, Elizabeth Marcella (mother) 8, 12, 16, 84

Henson, Heather (daughter) 63

Henson, Jane (wife). *See* Nebel, Jane

Henson, Jim (James Maury) *4, 15*

ambitions of 10–11, 16, 20–21, 27, 37, 72, 79, 88

and puppetry research 41–43, 78

as actor 12–13, 16, 22, 53

as a poet 12

as a puppeteer 13, 22, 26, 28–37, *39*, 40–42, 44–47, 49–50, *51*, 52–53, 56–58, 60, 62–63, *64*, 65–71, 73–79, *79*, 80, 82–84, *88*

as a world traveler 42–43, 68, 72, 74, 83

as drawing artist 9–10, 12, 22, 27–28, 37, 54

as jazz lover 37

awards 3, 43, 55, 65, 69–71, 82

birth 8

business matters 37–39, 41–42, 44, 50–53, 63, 72–74, 83

childhood 9–17

children 45–47, 50, 63, 74–75, 79, 80–81, 84–87

death 6, 84–85

death of brother 38

education 11–12, 15–18, 21–22, 27–28, 37, 42

efforts for child education 2, 61, 63, 66, *66*, 82, 87

film work 53–56, 61, 73–77, 77, 78, 80, *81*, 83–84

his effect on television and popular culture 1–3, 5, 7, 34, 41, 62, 65, 78, 87–89

homes of 8, 11, 44, 50, 53, 74, 83, 85

inspirations for work 6, 9–10

interest in technology 18, 29–30, 73, 75, 79

love interest 16, 29, 31

marriage 44–45, 79

methods of puppetry 32–37, 40–41, 73, 75

talks about himself and his work 5–6, 18, 29, 31, 36, 39, 42–43, 49–50, 53–55, 69, 87

television commercials
work 39–41, 44, 52–53,
60–61, 63
television work 5, 21,
25–26, 29–39, *39*, 40–44, 46,
49–50, 53, 57–58, 60–63, *64*,
65–73, 78–79, *79*, 80–82
time line 90–95
Henson, John (son) 53
Henson, Lisa (daughter)
45–46, 81
Henson, Paul Ransom
(father) 8, 10, 26–27, 84
Henson, Paul, Jr. (brother)
8–12, 27, 38
Henson Associates (HA) 72,
82
Henson Foundation 78
Hey, Cinderella! (television
program) 57–58, 60
The Hobbit (book) 75
Howdy Doody (puppet) 25
how to become a filmmaker
96–111
advancement 105–106
earnings 106–107
employers 103
exploration 102–103
high school/postsecondary
training 99–101
job overview 96–99
requirements 99–102
starting out 103–105

work environment/outlook
107–108
how to become a television
director 112–126
advancement 120
earnings 121
employers 119
exploration 118–119
high school/postsecondary
training 116–118
job overview 112–115
requirements 116–118
starting out 119–120
work environment/outlook
121–123
Hunt, Richard 58, 78
The Huntley-Brinkley Report
(television program) 30
Hurt, John 81

I
Icky Gunk (puppet) 35
Inga's Angle (puppet televi-
sion segment) 29

J
Jen (puppet) *77*
Jerry Mahoney (puppet) 25
The Jim Henson Hour (televi-
sion program) 83
Jim Henson Productions 82,
85–87
*Jim Henson's Mother Goose
Stories* (television series) 82

Jim Henson's Muppet Babies (television program) 78–79
Jim Henson's Muppet*Vision 3-D (film) 84
The Jimmy Dean Show (television program) 40, 52–53
John Denver and the Muppets: A Christmas Together (television program/record album) 73–74
John Denver and the Muppets: Rocky Mountain Holiday (television program) 78
Jones, Gordon 12–13
Juhl, Jerry 47, 49–51, 56, 88
Junior Good Morning Show (television program) 25–26

K
Kenworthy, Duncan 75
Kermit the Frog (puppet) 1, 15, *15*, 31, 35–36, 46, 58, *66*, 68, 70, 73, 77, 78, *88*
King Ploobis (puppet) 67
Kira (puppet) *77*
Kraft Television Theater (television program) 17
Kukla, Fran and Ollie (television program) 18–19, 25, 49
Kukla (puppet) 18–19

L
Labyrinth (film) 80, *81*
La Choy Dragon (puppet) 40–41

Lambchop (puppet) 25
Lazer, David 68
Lee, Will 62
Lewis, Shari 25
Life with Snarky Parker (television program) 19
Long, Loretta 63
Longhorn and Shorthorn (puppets) 26
The Lord of the Rings (book series) 75
Lovelady, John 58
Lucas, George 80

M
Mad, Mad World (television series pilot) 50
Mahna-Mahna (puppet) 68
Martin, Steve 73
McGrath, Bob 63
Michaels, Lorne 67
The Mighty Favog (puppet) 67
Minghella, Anthony 81
Miss Piggy (puppet) 1, *32*, 65, 68–70, 73, 77, 79, *88*
Mr. Hooper (live character) 62–63
Moldy Hay (puppet) 35
Mortimer Snerd (puppet) 14
Mullen, Kathryn 78
Muppet Christmas Carol (film) 86
A Muppet Family Christmas (television program) 83

The Muppet Movie (film) 73
The Muppet Musicians of Bremen (television program) 58
Muppets (puppets) 1–3, *32*, 36, 40–42, 46–47, 49–51, *51*, 52–54, 56–57, 60, 62–63, *64*, 65, 67–68, *70*, 73, 76–78, 82–86, *88*
The Muppets at Walt Disney World (television program) 84
Muppets From Space (film) 86
The Muppets Go to the Movies (television program) 78
The Muppet Shop 83
The Muppet Show (television program) 2–3, 31–32, 49, 68–70, *70*, 71–72, 75, 78, 83
Muppets Inc. 42
Muppets Magazine (magazine) 78
Muppets on Puppets (television program) 60
The Muppets Take Manhattan (film) 83
Muppets Tonight (television program) 86
The Muppets Valentine Special (television program) 65
Muppet Treasure Island (film) 86

Mushmellon (puppet) 35
Mystics (puppets) 76

N

Nebel, Jane (wife) 29, 31, 35, 38–39, 41–43, 46–47, 49–50, 57, 61, 63, 79, 84
Nelson, Jerry 58, 68, 78

O

Oliver "Ollie" J. Dragon (puppet) 19
Oscar the Grouch (puppet) 63, *64*
Our Place (television program) 57
Oz, Frank 47, *48*, 50–51, 68, 88–89
Oznowicz, Frank. *See* Oz, Frank
Oznowicz, Frances and Mike 47

P

Parkes, Gerry 78
Payne, Bob 43
Pierre the French Rat (puppet) 26
Prell, Karen 78
Professor Madcliffe (puppet) 35
Pryor, Richard 73
Punch and Judy (puppet show) 24
puppets, history of 22–25

R

"Rainbow Connection" (song) 73

Raposo, Joe 61

Red Ryder (radio program) 12

Robinson, Matt 63

Rowlf the Dog (puppet) 1, 40, 52–53, 57, 79

S

Sahlin, Don 49–52

Sam and Friends (television program) 30–31, 35–36, 38–39, *39*, 41–44, 49–50, 53

Sam (puppet) 30

Saturday Night Live (*SNL*) (television program) 67

Scooter (puppet) 68

Scott, T. Kermit 15–16

Scred (puppet) 67

Sgt. Floyd Pepper (puppet) 68

Sesame Street Presents: Follow that Bird (television program) 80

Sesame Street (television program) 2–3, 40, 58, 61–63, *64*, 65–67, 72, 83, 86

Sesame Street: 20 . . . And Still Counting (television program) 83

The Shadow (radio program) 12

Skeksis (puppet) 76

Star Wars: Episode V — The Empire Strikes Back (film) 75

Statler (puppet) 68

Stone, Jon 57, 60

The Storyteller (television series) 80–81, *81*, 82

Studio One (television program) 17

Sullivan, Ed 17

T

Tales from Muppetland (television program) 58

Tales of the Tinkerdee (television series pilot) 50

The Teenage Mutant Ninja Turtles (film) 83

The Teenage Mutant Ninja Turtles (television series) 83

Texaco Star Theater (television program) 18

"Three Little Pigs" (puppet television segment) 32

Tillstrom, Bill 18, 46, 49–50

The Time Machine (film) 49

Time Piece (film) 54–56

Toast of the Town (television program) 17

Today (television program) 46, 50

Toler, Sandra 16

Tolkien, J. R. R. 75
Tonight Show (television program) 30, 38

U

Ustinov, Peter 78

W

Wall, Russell 26
Walt Disney Company 84–86
Warren, Fran 19
Whedon, Tom 57
Whitmire, Steve 78
Wildcat Scratches (school magazine) 22
Wilkens and Wontkins (puppets) 39

Wilkens Coffee Company 39–40
Winchell, Paul 25
The Witches (film) 83
The Wizard of Oz (film) 11

Y

Yoda (film character) 75
Yorick (puppet) 31, 35–36, 46–47, 51
Youth '68 (television program) 56

Z

Zoot (puppet) 68

ABOUT THE AUTHOR

James Robert Parish, a former entertainment reporter, publicist, and book series editor, is the author of numerous biographies and reference books of the entertainment industry including *Gloria Estefan: Singer; Jennifer Lopez: Actor; Katie Couric: TV Newscaster; Stan Lee: Comic-Book Writer; Twyla Tharp: Choreographer; Denzel Washington: Actor; Halle Berry: Actor; Stephen King: Writer; Tom Hanks: Actor; Steven Spielberg: Filmmaker; Fiasco: A History of Hollywood's Iconic Flops; Katharine Hepburn: The Untold Story; The Hollywood Book of Scandals; Whitney Houston; The Hollywood Book of Love; Hollywood Divas; Hollywood Bad Boys; The Encyclopedia of Ethnic Groups in Hollywood; Jet Li; Gus Van Sant; The Hollywood Book of Death; Whoopi Goldberg; Rosie O'Donnell's Story; The Unofficial "Murder, She Wrote" Casebook; Today's Black Hollywood;* and *Let's Talk! America's Favorite TV Talk Show Hosts.*

Mr. Parish is a frequent on-camera interviewee on cable and network TV for documentaries on the performing arts both in the United States and in the United Kingdom. Mr. Parish resides in Studio City, California. Mr. Parish's website is http://www.jamesrobert parish.com.